MESSAGE OF THE SACRAMENTS

Monika K. Hellwig, Editor

Volume 4

Sign of Reconciliation and Conversion

The Sacrament of Penance for Our Times

by

Monika K. Hellwig

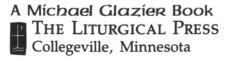

A Michael Glazier Book
THE LITURGICAL PRESS
Collegeville, Minnesota

A Michael Glazier Book published by The Liturgical Press

Cover design by Lillian Brulc

ISBN 0-8146-5272-7

4   5   6   7   8   9

Table of Contents

This book is dedicated to
my children
Erica, Michael and Carlos
in the hope that they will forgive me
for all that I have not been and done
for them
while it was being written
and that they will grow up to be
signs of reconciliation
extending friendship where there is racism,
joy where there is violence
and compassion where there is greed.

EDITOR'S PREFACE

This volume is one of the series of eight on *The Message of the Sacraments*. These volumes discuss the ritual practices and understanding and the individual sacraments of the Roman Catholic community. Each of the eight authors has set out to cover five aspects of the sacrament (or, in the first and last volumes, of the theme or issue under discussion). These are: first of all, the existential or experiential meaning of the sacrament in the context of secular human experience; what is known of the historical development of the sacrament; a theological exposition of the meaning, function and effect of the sacrament in the context of present official Catholic doctrinal positions; some pastoral reflections; and a projection of possible future developments in the practice and catechesis of the sacrament.

There is evident need of such a series of volumes to combine the established teaching and firm foundation in sacramental theology with the new situation of the post-Vatican II Church. Because the need is universal, this series is the joint effort of an international team of English-speaking authors. We have not invited any participants whose writing would need to be translated. While we hope that our series will be useful particularly to priests, permanent deacons, seminarians, and those professionally involved in sacramental and catechetical ministries, we also address ourselves confidently to the educated Catholic laity and to those outside the Roman Catholic communion who are interested in learning more about its life and thought. We have all tried to write so as to be easily understood by readers with little or no specialized preparation. We have all tried to deal with the tradition imaginatively but within the acceptable bounds of Catholic orthodoxy, in the firm conviction that that is the way in which we can be most helpful to our readers.

The Church seems to be poised today at a critical juncture in its history. Vatican II reopened long-standing questions about collegiality and participation in the life of the Church, including its sacramental actions, its doctrinal formulations and its government. The Council fostered a new critical awareness and raised hopes which the Church as a vast and complicated institution cannot satisfy without much confusion, conflict and delay. This makes ours a particularly trying and often frustrating time for those most seriously interested in the life of the Church and most deeply committed to it. It seems vitally important for constructive and authentically creative community participation in the shaping of the Church's future life, that a fuller understanding of the sacraments be widely disseminated in the Catholic community. We hope that many readers will begin with the volumes in this series and let themselves be guided into further reading with the bibliographies we offer at the ends of the chapters. We hope to communicate to our readers the sober optimism with which we have undertaken the study and thereby to contribute both to renewal and to reconciliation.

Monika K. Hellwig

ACKNOWLEDGEMENTS

My indebtedness to published sources is, of course, recorded in the footnotes of this book but my indebtedness to living contacts is much greater and I would like particularly to thank: (posthumously) Rev. Giuseppe Piantoni of the Verona Fathers for an understanding of the role of community charity in conversion; Rev. Thomas E. Clarke, S.J., of the Woodstock Center for the insights that the private penance tradition is coherent if one places confession within spiritual direction rather than the reverse and that the public penance tradition is coherent if the confession essential to conversion is of sinfulness rather than of specific sin; Rev. Paul Cioffi, S.J., of the Georgetown University Theology Department for an understanding of the role of *confessio laudis* as foundation for public penance in the patristic church; Rev. William McFadden, S.J., Chairman of the Department, for many good insights on conversion shared in eucharistic homilies; Rev. John C. Haughey, S.J., of the Woodstock Center for a veritable galaxy of luminous insights into Scripture and Christian experience shared with unfailing patience and good humor while this book was being written; Mrs. Eileen Daney Carzo of Michael Glazier, Inc. for more patience and understanding than any editor should ever be called upon to extend; my daughter, Erica, for fixing lunches and keeping her brothers in order so that I could continue writing; and last, but by no means least, Irene and Bill and Lisa McDonald who invited and entertained my three children for five days so that this book would finally be finished. Of all inadequacies, follies and obscurities in this book I unhesitatingly claim exclusive provenance.

INTRODUCTION

QUESTIONS WE HAVE TODAY

There is perhaps no corner of Catholic life and experience more fraught with questions and problems today than the sacrament of penance or reconciliation. The questions were becoming urgent long before the Second Vatican Council and diminishing participation was evident in most western countries even then. The reformed rites that came into existence after Vatican II were a response, at least in part, to the challenge of the contemporary questions and the challenge of the absences from the sacrament. Nevertheless, the reformed rites do not seem to have answered the Catholic people's nagging questions and problems because the absences have not grown less but seem rather to have grown to include many even of the devout.

It is a time for patience and for study and reflection, because it is necessary to try to understand the problem in all its historical, psychological and theological dimensions. It is a time for relentless honesty in facing the issues. But it is also a time for sober loyalty to the tradition, for it would be all too easy to lose a heritage that has been built out of the cumulative wisdom of the centuries by Christian peoples deeply committed to the living of their faith. It is the intent of this volume to set out the issues as frankly as possible and to draw on the history of the community, its present experience and its theology and doctrine in quest of resources for constructive solutions to the problems.

There seem to be three aspects or factors in one's participation in the sacrament of penance. These are the sense of sinfulness and need of reconciliation and conversion; the understanding of mediation and especially of the role of ordained priests in the Catholic community; and the perception and interpretation of the rites themselves. In each of these factors there are some open or hidden conflicts for Catholics today. This introduction will set out briefly what those conflicts seem to be. Subsequent chapters attempt in some measure to resolve them.

There can be no coherence or authenticity in the sacrament of penance where there is no spontaneous and practical sense of sinfulness and the need for reconciliation and conversion. This is partly a matter of experience, sensitivity and self-knowledge, and partly a matter of understanding what is meant by sin. Both of these present a problem today. People's experience, sensitivity and self-knowledge are very much influenced by the society and culture in which they live. In our culture there is a strong bias against negative feelings and evaluations of oneself, as witnessed by constant exhortations from "pop" psychologists to think positively, to "think big", to think "you can do it", to think "I'm O.K., you're O.K." or (humorously) "I'm O.K., you're not so hot" and so forth. Moreover, there is a certain bias in the culture against developing sensitivity to one's own impact on others simply because of the strong emphasis on competition which carries with it the need for self-promotion based on deeply rooted convictions that one "deserves" to be promoted and to accumulate goods, power and status at others' expense.

This pressure from the culture around us meets with an experience of the sacrament of penance which is usually too shallow and empty to counter it. First of all, most Catholics have met the sacrament of penance for the first time and have had their only serious instruction in it in circumstances where it appeared simply as part of the process of initiation into the community of worship, a sort of "rite of passage" that must be undergone to prove maturity for the privilege of first holy communion in the Eucharist. Thus it was not connected with a sense of sinfulness or need of reconciliation or conversion but with a sense of promotion to a higher status by an ordeal closely related to examinations, vaccinations and other more or less frightening gateways into increasing maturity. This alone would tend to produce a certain inauthenticity, but it has been matched for many people with an inadequate understanding of sin. In order to pass the promotion ordeal one had to be able to recite a list of transgressions that sounded appropriate to the confessional. One had to do it on a schedule determined by organizational exigences that bore no relation to one's personal experience, behavior or self-awareness. In most cases people did this early in childhood. Their understanding of sin was necessarily one of transgressions against explicit commands (more usually against prohibitions) by particular actions. Sin in other words was simply breaking the rules set by lawfully constituted authority.

Most adults at some time or other experience the inadequacy of such a concept of sin. It seems to have so little to do with the real issues in life. The real issues are never quite so clearly black and white. What is good is not always what is commanded by lawfully constituted authority, nor is it always neatly blueprinted beforehand. Moreover, the real issues are so much more subtle. Seldom are they contained in particular actions of particular individuals. More generally they are entangled in values and structures of society, in complex patterns of inter-personal relations, in attitudes and assumptions taken for granted and therefore often hidden from those who hold them. This alone leads to the acute sense of unreality that many Catholics have today concerning the sacrament of penance.

However, there is yet another dimension of the sense of unreality. There is a growing caution concerning the attribution of personal guilt in our society. Many feel that even notorious criminals should not be blamed or punished but should be diagnosed, treated and rehabilitated as mentally sick people suffering these aberrations of conduct for reasons ultimately quite beyond their control. We are becoming more and more conscious of hereditary and environmental factors that tend to shape a person's life and behavior in acceptable or unacceptable, constructive or destructive patterns. We are loath to attribute personal guilt. At the same time we have grown up with explicit or implicit definitions of sin which are centered upon the notion of personal responsibility and freedom of choice and guilt. To approach individual confession with this concept of sin and the concept of the sacrament sketched above is a problem to anyone with the contemporary awareness of the forces conditioning behavior. What is supposedly being attempted is futile, because neither penitent nor confessor is in a position to make the determinations that would correctly define sin in the concrete and therefore provide the matter of the sacrament. There is an uneasy sense of going through an empty formality and making the sacred trivial and ridiculous.

Many Catholics who do not really want to abandon their tradition nevertheless feel this overwhelming sense of triviality and desecration. They either continue to frequent the sacrament in a kind of quiet desperation because they know it must have meaning although they are not finding it, or else they find one day that without ever having quite intended it they have in fact abandoned the practice of the sacrament and are not in a position, according to their present understanding, to resume that practice. Often they are bewildered and distressed by this state of affairs.

The above problems are intimately intertwined with the understanding of mediation — the mediation of the sacrament and more particularly of the one who administers the sacrament. It raises acute problems and questions concerning the role of the ordained priest in the Catholic community. Many Catholics have been accustomed to think of the priest as the privileged dispenser of God's favors and the chosen oracle of God's judgments. If sin means breaking the rules, the priest is not only official judge as to whether the rules have been broken and how serious the transgression is but also the one designated to grant indemnity and to specify the conditions.

Once the legalistic concept of sin breaks down, there are new questions about the role of the priest in the sacrament of penance. When people become aware of hatred, jealousy, envy or resentment in their lives they are more likely to turn to a psychoanalyst than to the sacrament of penance. When they become aware of racism, sexism or other prejudices, they are more likely to turn to sensitivity training or special workshops. When they begin to realize the extent of social injustice in which they are somehow implicated, they may join organizations, attend lectures, or participate in group discussions suggesting possible and appropriate action or sharing experiences of simplifying life-styles and so forth. When there is tension and quarrelling in the family they are more likely to go to a marriage counselor. Even if they are in quest of a Christian conversion in their lives they are more likely to join a prayer group, a bible study circle, a basic community. Increasingly, it seems, when they want to decide with a clear conscience what to do in matters such as birth-control, they are more likely to turn to someone else with the same type of marital situation than to take their questions of conscience into the confessional.

For Catholics of our time, the sacrament of penance is so inextricably and unquestioningly bound up with their understanding of the role of the priest that the emergence of other experts in all these fields, of other channels for resolving such problems, seems to raise the question not only of defining the specific competence of the priest but also of determining whether there is any meaning left in the sacrament of penance. It may be objected that none of the above relationships explicitly invokes God or the relation of the human person to God. It may also be objected that the above considerations entirely by-pass the question of grace. This is true on both counts, but the objection somehow begs the question. The contemporary difficulties are based on an experience of life that yields a different perception of the relation between nature and grace than that which is assumed by the objection. Nature and grace are not seen as separate and mutually exclusive categories but as interpenetrating within a single reality of human experience and not sharply differentiated within that experience. The relationship of the human person with God is seen, quite properly, as inseparable from the ordinary problems of living everyday life.

Perhaps it would be an even more correct reading of the contemporary consciousness of the Catholic laity in our own culture to say that there seems to be an uneasy coexistence of two dissociated and irreconcilable perceptions, often within the same individual, of the relationship to God as the source, meaning and goal of human life. There is on the one hand the "catechism God", rather literally personal, in fact three rather literal persons, the Supreme Being presiding over a kind of pyramid of beings, ruling, judging, rewarding and punishing, less obviously in "this life" but with great surety in the hereafter. On this life's side of the pyramid, priests and sacraments are very securely ensconced as mediating the rules, judgements, rewards and punishments. If their relevance and effects are not evident they are nevertheless accepted on hearsay, because we know we do not see the hereafter side of the pyramid on which all will be plain, permanent and inescapable. This God and this understanding inspire fear of transgression of apparently arbitrary rules and therefore foster the need of ritual reassurance by people who officially know and officially have some power over the rules.

On the other hand, in the experience of contemporary Catholics there is at the same time another perception of God. This God is frighteningly unlike the catechism God, elusive, more impersonal than personal in the experience of the believer, more absent than present and in that scant presence more within self-awareness and interpersonal relationships than over against them, powerful only in a sense that we do not easily recognize as power and even then powerful rather within human freedom than over or alongside of it. This God of contemporary experience is such as to leave individuals and societies with full responsibility and all the risks of real freedom. This God invalidates all ritual assurances in the name of common sense experience.

Such a divided sense of God seems often to result in ambivalence, bewilderment and anger concerning the judgmental role of the priest confessor. It raises questions concerning the force of his "binding and loosing" power before God and before the penitent's own conscience. Penitents who exercise some measure of freedom of conscience may have some anxiety concerning the validity of the absolution given in the sacrament. At the least they have a certain sense that it is vaguely dishonest or inauthentic and they feel burdened by this. On the other hand, penitents who take what they deem to be the safer option of exercising no freedom of conscience and making, in effect, no concrete judgments of their own in moral choices, seem to feel increasingly oppressed and bullied and seem very frequently to come to a point at which the tension between their own spontaneous judgments and the "official" verdict becomes intolerable. Some of the angriest, bitterest "former" Catholics tell the story of their alienation with reference to this type of situation.

The example most frequently cited is the question of the morality of contraceptive practices within a marriage. This is a question in which the conflict between the couple's own sincere and sober assessment of what is right in the concrete situation and the "official" verdict soon becomes particularly desperate because of the interpersonal dynamics within the marriage and because of the overwhelming realization that the "official" verdict has been concluded by those who have no direct experience of those dynamics and are not vulnerable to experience in the matter. The matter is dangerously exacerbated in those dioceses and situations in which confessors routinely question penitents about their sexual practices and about the matter of contraception in particular before giving absolution, even when the content of the confession has made no reference to such subject matter. There is a growing sense of restlessness and unjust domination among devout and loyal Catholics who want to frequent the sacrament but feel that such questioning is an attempt to usurp their God-given conscience and crush any initiative to make responsible personal judgments as adults. There is a growing resentment in the realization that such attempts to reduce adults to childish deprivation of personal responsibility is driving out of the Catholic Church good Christians who very much want to be fully participant in it.

The least conflict and tension in the role of the priest and the role of official Church mediation in general seems to be felt by those who are fortunately placed so as to have a very wide choice of confessors and who have been able to find long-term regular confessors to whom they voluntarily open their lives, thoughts, doubts and aspirations for continuing spiritual guidance. This happens when people have easy access to monasteries or large religious houses and institutions. It also happens in many large cities but then usually only for the highly educated who are also leisured. These tend to be the elderly and the single without family responsibilities and therefore those least likely to be caught in the situation described above.

However, even among persons so fortunately placed the question of the mediating role of the ordained priest is sometimes a practical one. A small but significantly growing minority of such people is turning for spiritual guidance to religious women, to non-ordained religious men, and to competent lay men and women. The people who do this have made the choice because they were convinced they had found those who could best mediate the guidance of the Spirit in their lives and therefore in fidelity to the call of the Spirit they turned to these guides. In this way the practice of lay confession, which has a respectable history in the Church as will be mentioned later in this volume, is slowly reasserting itself alongside of the canonically regulated, officially sacramental confession to designated priests. People who have sought out non-ordained guides often go to them regularly to make a very complete "manifestation of conscience", that is a confession not only of sin and sinfulness, but of their temptations, aspirations and questions, of

their practices and experiences of prayer, their understanding of their personal and social responsibilities and so
forth. In such cases there can not but be an awareness that
such a confession is sacramental in the broader sense of the
word. It effects the grace of repentance and continuing
conversion which it signifies by the mediation that links the
penitent to the person and action of Jesus who entrusted his
followers with the task of helping one another in reconciliation and conversion. But this then raises the question of the
relationship between the two kinds of sacramentality.

The third area of contemporary questions concerning the
sacrament of penance has to do with the rites themselves. It
has to do with both the theory and the practice of these rites.
Most frequently heard is the question of why it should be
necessary to make an individual confession in order to
receive absolution when there are now officially three rites
of the sacrament of penance itself besides the reconciliation
rites within the Eucharist.[1] The question arises because the
new ritual includes not only communal celebration in which
individual confessions are inserted, and separate reconciliation of individual penitents privately, but it also contains a
third rite consisting of communal celebration with general
absolution (that is, without individual confessions), which is
described as a normal and solemn celebration of the sacrament of penance, though limited to "cases provided for in
the law". Further inquiry then reveals that this apparently
innocuous phrase is so restrictive that the third rite is not
rightly seen as a normal celebration at all.[2] Yet once it is
known that such a rite exists in the ritual, many Catholic
people begin to feel that the question of the necessity of an
individual and specific confession becomes one of the great-

[1] The full texts of these rites along with the instructions for celebrating them are
available in the form approved for use in dioceses of the U.S. in *The Rite of
Penance* (N.Y.: Catholic Book Publishing Company, 1975).

[2] *Ibid.,* pp. 24-25, sections 31-34. The historical reasons for the restrictions are set
out by Frederick R. McManus, in *The Rite of Penance: Commentaries, vol.
I.: Understanding the Document,* by Ralph Keifer and Frederick R. McManus
(Washington, D.C.: Liturgical Conference, 1975), pp. 111-114.

est urgency and importance that cannot easily be put aside or postponed.

Behind this more obvious question lies another concerning the rites of the sacrament of penance, namely, what are the constitutive elements of the sacrament and which if any of them is central. Is it the repentance or the confession of sin that is crucial in complementarity with the absolution, and is specific rather than generic confession of sin in some way essential to the sacrament? This question demands a very careful consideration of the history of the sacrament, that is, the history both of its practice and of its theology. The question is important not only in determining what is properly to be considered the sacrament of penance in the strict sense and what is not properly so considered though it may indeed be a reconciliation rite. It is important to ask this question also in order to conduct the sacrament in such a way that it may be fully significant and effective, a matter in which there is at present widespread dissatisfaction.

This question in turn leads to another which has to do with the relationships and distinctions between various sacramental rites of reconciliation and conversion, more especially those of baptism, penance, anointing of the sick and Eucharist. Though this question is not so frequently asked, it is the next logical step that follows when one deals with the foregoing ones. This question has a traditional formulation in which it has long been considered, namely, the quest to isolate or determine the "specific sacramental grace" of each sacrament. Again, it is helpful to pursue this question, not only to validate penance as a separate sacrament, but in order to understand how to celebrate it significantly and effectively.[3]

It is the intent of this volume to lay out these questions in greater detail in the following chapters, to survey the resour-

---

[3]The perception and analysis of contemporary questions as presented in this introduction are based upon personal conversations with large numbers of Catholics from various parts of the English speaking world, including those who still confess and those who do not, those who still consider themselves Church members and those who profess themselves tentatively or decisively alienated.

ces of the tradition for their solution, briefly giving references to monographs and more comprehensive works where they may be studied in detail, and to propose a theological interpretation of the sacrament of penance that is orthodox within the Roman Catholic tradition as well as pastorally helpful.

Recommended Reading

Nathan Mitchell, OSB, ed., *The Rite of Penance: Commentaries, Vol. 3: Background and Directions.* (Washington, D.C.: The Liturgical Conference, 1978).

Edward Schillebeeckx, O.P. ed. *Sacramental Reconciliation* (N.Y.: Herder, 1971).

Joseph Martos, *Doors to the Sacred* (N.Y.: Doubleday, 1981). Ch. IX, Penance, pp. 307-364,

An Anglican perspective on some of the above questions is offered in: Kenneth Leech, *Soul Friend: A Study of Spirituality* (London: Sheldon Press, 1977).

A Protestant perspective is offered in: Richard J. Foster, *Celebration of Discipline: Path to Spiritual Growth* (N.Y. and London: Harper & Row, 1978), Part III. The Corporate Disciplines, pp. 175-172.

CHAPTER I

SIN, REPENTANCE AND CONVERSION

Throughout the centuries, the Church has had many rituals celebrating repentance and conversion. In fact, even before the Christian era, the history of Israel is full of such rituals, many of which are described for us in the Hebrew Scriptures.[1] The reason for the rituals is of course that repentance and conversion are themselves a central theme of the Hebrew and Christian Scriptures and of our whole religious history in the Jewish and Christian communities. The good news that is preached as the central Christian message is that God welcomes back in reconciliation all who turn to him and that this gives meaning, purpose, integration, joy to the individual, the community, and the creation as a whole. The transcendent God reaches deeply and intimately into his creation in the person of Jesus Christ and by the inner power of the Holy Spirit, making such a turning possible.

In one sense then, the Church as a whole is the instrument to make that turning possible for its members and for the world. In other words, the Church is a sacrament (or effective sign) of salvation which means a sacrament of repentance and conversion. Its central act, the Eucharist, is a ritual of reconciliation and return and so are, in one way or

---

[1] Cf. Jean Giblet, "Repentance — Conversion", in *Dictionary of Biblical Theology*, ed. X. Leon-Dufour (N.Y.: Desclee, 1967), pp. 430-434.

another, most of its activities and celebrations. The sacrament of penance can only be understood in this context. It can be meaningful only if there is an authentic understanding of the pervasive need to "turn". In other words, the meaning of the sacrament of penance is dependent upon an understanding of the meaning of sin.

Although the Greek text of the New Testament uses the word, *metanoia*, for repentance, a word that has the sense of changing one's mind, the basic Hebrew word apparently favored by Jesus is *shuv*. Although this can mean "again", there is a more concretely physical sense of returning, retracing one's steps, reversing one's direction. It suggests a state of affairs in which someone has been travelling in the wrong direction and therefore moving farther and farther away from the goal. By using the image of returning to God, retracing one's steps to come back to God, the Bible gives an implicit definition of sin. Sin appears as the condition or state of being focussed on goals other than God, finding meaning in life without ultimate reference to God.

Perhaps the most striking biblical illustration of this is Jesus' parable of the prodigal younger son (Lk. 15:11-32). The sinner is represented as having travelled away from home, away from the Father, having squandered his inheritance until finally he realizes that he is terribly alienated in an utterly inauthentic and unsatisfying existence. An aspect of the parable that is very interesting is that according to the property laws and inheritance customs of the time the younger son had done something illicit though not at all unusual. By the Hebrew law the father could convey the ownership of the younger son's one-third share of inheritance during his lifetime but with all sorts of safeguards to prevent its being sold or the income from it being spent against the father's approval. Nevertheless, at the times when emigration seemed an attractive alternative to the poverty of Palestine, it was not unknown for sons to want and obtain their inheritance in cash and emigrate to cities of the *diaspora* (the dispersed communities of Jews who lived outside the Holy Land).

Several facts are of great interest in the analogy from contemporary life that Jesus chose in order to make his point. The issue is one of independence — not of freedom so much as of independence. According to the traditional law it was an illegitimate independence that undermined life according to the covenant. The father of the story, like the actual fathers of the time, nevertheless respects the boy's freedom and allows him to "seek his fortune" by asserting independence of law and custom in order to emigrate. The father evidently anticipates what will happen but waits — with great longing, one surmises, from the alertness with which he sees him even from a long way off and runs toward him when he returns. Meanwhile, no one needs to upbraid the son and tell him how alienated he is. He knows that from the way his life is falling apart; he experiences not only hunger and material deprivation but the degradation of a Jew employed as a swineherd (pigs being unclean according to the law) and the meaninglessness of the life to which he has been reduced. The story has him "coming to himself" or "coming to his senses", a Hebrew expression for repentance. Coming to himself, his impulse is to return, to retrace his steps, to go home to his father.[2]

The repentance and the returning in this story do not seem to refer to particular transgressions, but to the basic condition of being away from the father's house in a false assertion of independence. What he repents is not so much an act or even a series of acts as a condition, a state of affairs, an outlook on life, a total personal orientation. The question as to his degree of personal culpability is not even raised, much less any question of having to itemize his unlawful acts during his absence. His father cuts him off in his attempt to confess his sin, because it is his mere return that makes the father's reconciling love effective.

The second part of this story is also a story of sinfulness encountering the reconciling love of the father. The elder

[2]For an explanation of this parable in detail, *cf.* Joachim Jeremias, *Rediscovering the Parables* (N.Y.: Scribners, 1966), pp. 97-105; and *Parables* by Madeleine Boucher (Wilmington, Del.: Michael Glazier Inc., 1981)

son is to all appearances living in the father's house in willing dependence on him, attending his wishes. Yet the scandal taken at the father's inexhaustible compassion is, so to speak, diagnostic of the real personal orientation which is one of self-righteousness. In a sense, he is asserting as much illegitimate independence as the younger son, but more subtly. The father speaks to him with the same compassion and love but he is not able to perceive that. There is a sense in which, contrary to appearances, he is not living in the father's house nor attuned to the father's will. In fact, he finds the father's judgment flawed and his outlook unfair and ridiculous. He is as alienated as his brother but is unable to see that.

In its gospel context, this second part of the story is a defense of the actions of Jesus himself, for Jesus is shown as turning continually to the poor, the disreputable, the obviously sinful. Regularly the Gospels show us the respectable taking offense because Jesus declares the Kingdom of Heaven open to such outcasts on the same terms as it is opened to the apparently righteous. It is not only the contemporaries of Jesus, however, who take scandal at this. Throughout history the respectable, the law-abiding, the devout confidently place themselves in a different category from the obviously sinful, and would like to maintain the exclusion of the latter from the privileged before God. Again and again human piety identifies sin with lawbreaking and, more particularly, the dramatic acts of destruction and rebellion, while failing to see sin in the fundamental stance of "knowing better than God" and not needing to live in creaturely dependence on God. Again and again human piety fails to see the distorted values and structures and expectations of human society which in fact make all human persons sinners, needy and poor before the consuming holiness and love of God. Human piety tends rather to divide people into two categories, the sinners and the just. It even claims to be able to distinguish between them. All this is radically challenged by Jesus in the second half of the story which juxtaposes the petty, judgmental meanness of the respectable elder brother with the indiscriminately welcoming compassion of the father.

Paul, reflecting on the radical challenge of this vision of Jesus, refers everything back to the Hebrew story of the fall of Adam in the garden (Gen. 3; Rom. 5). The story of the sin of Adam as given in the book of Genesis is, of course, a story of disobedience to an explicit command of God. But the implications are much broader and deeper than that, when one considers what the temptation was. It was to eat of the fruit so as to be like God, determining good and evil. In the temptation God is represented as an oppressor restricting human freedom and human becoming. The relationship of dependence on God is presented as a diminishment of what is human; and independence from God, by the snatching of the forbidden fruit, is presented as the great liberation that opens the way to fulfillment. The matter becomes clearer yet when one considers who the tempter was. The extra-biblical stories fill in the identity of the tempter as that of the "fallen angel", the primordial rebel spirit, who has gone forth from God's heaven with the slogan, "I will not serve", who will not be creature, who will not bend his being to be for another.

Hence the story of Adam's eating of the fruit in the garden is not at all a fanciful tale about an arbitrary test situation. It is a vivid tableau of the human situation now as always — balanced between the invitation to a more than creaturely intimacy with God on the one hand and a less than creaturely, self-defeating bid for unsituated freedom in independence of God on the other. The irony of the temptation is that, as told in the first creation account, the human person is indeed made to be in the likeness of God (Gen. 1:26-27); and, as told in the second creation account, God breathes his own breath into the human person sparking human life that is brought into dialogue with God himself and into a co-creative relationship to the earth and all the creatures in it (Gen. 2:7-20). It is evidently not sin in this story to desire to be like God but to desire to be as gods in independence of the true God.

Both the extra-biblical story of the fallen angel and the biblical story of Adam are somehow analogous to the story Jesus told of the younger son. In each of them there is a going forth from the Father's house, a demand for independence and a journey to disaster. The point that Paul makes (Rom. 5) is that the resultant situation of disaster is the human situation in which we all find ourselves, from which we all need to be rescued — a task to which the Law is inadequate and which only the grace of Christ can accomplish. Paul is justified, of course, in his position by the fact that the preaching of Jesus clearly implies that all are sinners.[3] From this position in the New Testament there developed the whole Catholic doctrine of "original sin".[4]

When we say, therefore, that the good news of the Christian gospel is that God not only welcomes back in reconciliation with himself all who turn from their sin to retrace their steps to him but that He also makes this turning possible in the first place by His outreach through the person of Jesus and the inner power of the Spirit, the sin intended in this statement is not primarily a collective noun for strings of individual transgressions. These latter are rather symptomatic of a universal condition of human persons and societies. It is a condition of disorientation, of lack of true center and focus.[5] In the stories of the angelic fall and of the fall of

[3]An excellent and insightful chapter on the implications of the universality of sin, written from a Lutheran point of view and well worth study by Catholic readers is Chapter 4 in *The Faith of the Christian Church* by Gustav Aulèn (Philadelphia: Fortress Press, 1960), pp. 231-292.

[4]For the New Testament teaching on the sin of Adam see: *The Biblical Doctrine of Original Sin* by René Dubarle (N.Y.: Herder, 1965) and *Pauline Theology: A Brief Sketch* by Joseph A. Fitzmeyer (Englewood Cliffs: Prentice-Hall, 1967), pp. 53-60.

[5]For the development of the doctrine of original sin in Catholic tradition and its implications for our understanding see *Man and Sin* by Piet Schoonenberg (Notre Dame, Inc.: University of Notre Dame Press, 1965), especially Part IV, pp. 124-199. For early developments in detail, including the influence of non-biblical Jewish thought, see *The Sources of the Doctrine of the Fall and Original Sin* by F.R. Tennant (N.Y.: Schocken, 1968). The biblical parts of this book should be read in the awareness that it was first published in 1903 and thus preceded much of modern scripture scholarship. Nevertheless, the author's interests and concern

Adam, as in the story of the wayward younger son, it is in the falling apart of the harmony of the creation and of creaturely existence that the state of sin is revealed. It is in suffering and frustration and meaninglessness that the realization of a fundamental state of alienation rushes in if allowed to do so.

Much of human culture, of course, is organized precisely to avoid this by anaesthetizing people, so to speak, against the deeper levels of experience. We do this by the multiplicity of goals, commitments, entertainments and distractions. We do it by civil structures of law and order whereby we manage to create a semblance of harmony in our lives and societies, which is really a rather thin veneer and often breaks down. When it breaks down, we remake the laws and structures or apply them more stringently, especially against the poor, the powerless, the oppressed, convincing ourselves all the while that the laws ought to work and that failures are quite accidental. Unfortunately we are also able to anaesthetize ourselves with beliefs and practices of religion which look as though they were attuned to God's creative and redemptive will but which are really ways of remaining at a distance from the Father's house and rule, maintaining a "safe" distance by confining the exigence of God in churchiness and religiosity with the hidden motive of preventing it from permeating the real substance of our lives.

It is at the moments where our human culture breaks down that there explodes in our faces the emptiness and the absence of God as the central focus in an existence that has become self-directed and disoriented. Most obvious of these moments is death. Death poses inescapably the fundamental question about the meaning and ultimate purpose of our lives.[6] It mediates the love of God to us in its most exigent form. Because death is known beforehand to be the inevita-

speak directly to contemporary experience, and he presents a very thorough survey of the Church Fathers on the topic.

[6]See: *On the Theology of Death* by Karl Rahner (N.Y.: Seabury, 1973); and *The Mystery of Death* by Ladislaus Boros (N.Y.: Herder, 1965).

ble outcome of our lives, it approaches as a redeeming judgment on our spendthrift and disoriented existence. There are other moments, such as painful and debilitating illness, unmanageable depression and anxiety, loneliness, misunderstandings with friends, the explosion of crime in a society, the outbreak of terrible wars which none of the parties wants though none will compromise on the self-interests at stake, and so forth.

These are moments at which the culture patterns cannot hide the fact that the human situation is one of need and vulnerability and dependence. They are moments at which the culture patterns we have built up can no longer conceal reliance on false securities such as money, fame and respectability. In these moments the hollow emptiness is no longer concealed by trivial distractions such as sports and entertainments and "keeping up with the Joneses". They are moments at which we discover a certain disorientation and experience this disorientation as bitter exile from our authentic existence. But for this very reason they may be times of grace and opportunity because the possibility of turning becomes evident in a desperate situation in which there is little or nothing to lose. Whether we know it or not, we are all born and raised in a world whose values and laws and structures and respectabilities are distorted. We are all in some measure caught in the disorientation of false values. Therefore we are all liable to be challenged to "turn" by such moments of grace and opportunity.

The moments of grace and opportunity of conversion must, however, be recognized and welcomed in order to be effective. Hence the role of the stories, the doctrines and the rituals that are concerned with sin, repentance and conversion. The purpose of all three is to bring about an awareness and recognition of sin in oneself and in one's society, and to foster a vivid experience of the possibilities and pathways of repentance, conversion and reconciliation. Both aspects of this — the recognition of sin and the realization of the possibility of conversion — arise spontaneously out of a growing consciousness of the overwhelming goodness of

God and the pervasive power of the divine compassion in the world. Therefore the stories must be told, the doctrines explained and the rituals celebrated in such a way that their main message is the goodness and compassion of God and that all else flows from it.

In this context, sin can never be reduced to the breaking of rules or commandments. It can not even be reduced to a collectivity of specific, discrete destructive deeds. Sin is deliberate or unrecognized detachment from God, orientation of human striving away from God. It is the placing of ultimate trust in anything other than God, even the placing of trust in moral behavior or good conduct according to the Law of God (inasmuch as we are ever able really to know such a law). This, of course, is why the letters of Paul in the New Testament contain such harsh sayings about the impossibility of salvation by the law. The other side of the impossibility of salvation by the law is the understanding that Christian faith has of the role of Jesus in relation to sin, conversion and reconciliation.

In the eyes of Christian faith Jesus is, in the first place, the revelation and expression among us of the indomitable love and compassion of God reaching into the last strongholds of resistance, the innermost fortresses of obstinacy against the redeeming forgiveness in which God reconciles all to Himself. Christian faith focuses especially on the death of Jesus, a death freely chosen because he himself discerned it as the redemptive path among the options that a sinful and disoriented world left him. It is this death that emerges so clearly as the ultimate self-expression of love. It is the love of the Father by Jesus in which all the poor and needy and suffering and disoriented of the world are spontaneously and unconditionally included. But it is also the love that the Father has for Jesus that is manifested in the loving response of Jesus. It is the fully effective love of the Father for him and in him that transfigures him to dazzling realizations of the possibilities of being human in the image and likeness of God. This love of the Father for Jesus reaches out in him and through him to the whole disoriented, alienated, suffering world, simply by virtue of the kind of man Jesus has come to be — focused on the Father in total trust and simplicity and therefore free for others in a total self-gift of compassion and an unflinching, unfailing discernment of the state of orientation or disorientation, of the resistances and the openings for conversion in others.

Christian tradition has expressed this in another way in speaking of the sinlessness of Jesus. This sinlessness of Jesus certainly is not asserted in the sense that according to the existing categories of law and religion Jesus did not transgress. Indeed his contemporaries observed many such transgressions and took scandal at them — breaking of the Sabbath, of ritual purification laws and so forth. What Christian faith asserts about Jesus is rather this, that in Jesus we discover the inadequacy and inappropriateness of all our concepts of sin and conversion. In him we see what human life is intended to be in the image and likeness of God. Therefore in him we have a revelation of what is sinful in the existing patterns of human life and values and expectations, and it is a startling revelation indicating much that we would be inclined to take rather for virtue than for sin. The crucifixion of Jesus is presented to us in Scripture and tradition like a vast tableau interpreting all of human life and society and history in relation to the Word and Spirit of God. In that tableau the notorious sinners on whom society has heaped all its guilt are quite ambivalently placed, being frequently ready hearers of the redeeming Word, although there is no doubt that they are indeed sinners. The ordinary and the pious people are not significantly differently placed from the notorious sinners. But the powers, the respectable and apparently trustworthy institutions and structures of the society, both civil and religious, are all most decisively and clearly ranged against Jesus as the redeeming Word of God uttered in our midst.

All this speaks a message about the nature of sin that is very hard to grasp. It asks for a far more radical faith and trust than most of us are ready to make for most of our lives.[7] It suggests that to be a follower of Jesus, to have authentic fellowship with him, to be oriented to the Father as he is, is indeed a very radical counter-cultural stance. That is to say, it requires growth to a maturity in faith in which judgments can really be made from inner conviction according to the mind and heart of Jesus and under the impulse of the Spirit, in great freedom from the need for reassurance by the respectabilities and guarantees of human social structures, because none of these is worthy of ultimate trust. The message about the nature of sin and the nature of conversion to holiness of life is certainly that these are discerned in the light of one final principle, namely Jesus in person, and not in the light of any codifiable law. Therefore the discernment is a lifelong, centuries long, continuing and unending journey of discovery. Hence the need for a continuing quest for discernment and openness to conversion within the Christian life. This in turn means a need for stories, doctrines and rituals that foster a pattern of growth and association and mutual help in the quest.

At the very source and center of such activity is, of course, the need to embody, to make present, the love of God expressed in human loving, cherishing, fostering. Jesus is, in the first place, the embodiment of the divine love humanly in the world.[8] But we, the community of his followers in different times and places, are called to be the embodiment of the embodiment which is Jesus, and therefore called to be the experience of the love of God humanly expressed in which sin is revealed and conversion and reconciliation are discovered to be possible. In other words, a practical task of reconciliation facilitating conversions is at the heart of the whole enterprise which we call Church. More fundamental

---

[7] *Cf. Has Sin Changed?* by Sean Fagan (Wilmington, Del: Michael Glazier, 1977), *passim* but especially Chapters 1, 2 and 6.

[8] *Cf.* The basic thesis of Edward Schillebeeckx in *Christ the Sacrament of the Encounter with God* (N.Y.: Sheed & Ward, 1963), especially Chapter 1, pp. 7-45. The idea is also basic in the thinking of Karl Rahner; see, *e.g.* "On the Theology of the Incarnation", *Theological Investigations,* Vol. IV (Baltimore: Helicon, 1966), pp. 105-120.

than any of the obviously religious or "churchy" activities, more fundamental than hierarchic or clerical functions, more fundamental than institutional unity and doctrinal orthodoxy and continuity, is the task of being community, the task of a genuine, practical, far-reaching sharing of life and resources and ideals and mutual respect and support. This is the basic channel by which the grace of God is communicated and becomes effective in rescuing each of us and all of us from our alienation, reconciling us with our true source and goal and center which is God (2 Cor. 5:16-21).

Church, then, must be the reconciliation, the welcome home of the Father expressed by the family of God, which makes the repentance and conversion possible. For it is not the other way around. God does not forgive us and reconcile us to himself because we have repented and converted (that is, turned ourselves around). Rather we are enabled to repent, to come to ourselves or come to our senses, precisely because God is irrevocably welcoming, imperturbably forgiving, indestructibly reconciling. We see this, of course, in our immediate experience of the covenant of creation — in sunrise, in spring, in germinating of seeds and birth of children, in healing of wounds and mending of bones and fresh rains after a long drought and the deep calm after a violent storm. We know it also in our intimate experience of the covenant of Noah, the covenant of conscience with God who makes peace in the heavens and grants it also on earth to all who live in quest of truth, goodness and beauty — in the faithful love of spouses, the self-sacrificing care of parents, the staunch loyalty of friends, the justice of those who build good societies, the courage of rescue squads, the sensitivity of peacemakers and the compassion of healers. And yet, because we indubitably live in a history of ambivalence where all that is good is also interlaced with the corroding consequences of evil deeds and fraught with distortion and illusion, we have need further of the healing covenant of God's special and redemptive intervention in our sinful history, in order even to be able to see beyond doubt and equivocation that God is indeed welcoming, forgiving and reconciling.

Church is that embodiment of God's compassion which makes the compassion quite tangible in the context of confusion and ambivalence which is the state of sin in the world. But this embodiment cannot be institutionally guaranteed, even by the best structures, the most appropriate laws. Hence our trust cannot be in the law but only in merciful love. This is true not only in relation to the law of Moses in the covenant of Israel. It is also true that salvation is not by the law of Christ but by the loving compassion of Christ, not by the law of the Church but by the welcome and reconciliation mediated in the community, embodying Christ as the compassion of God. The history of the Church and its practices of reconciliation shows a long and complicated struggle in the Christian community to realize this and grow to the full stature of Christ as the true elder brother who understands the compassion of the Father and the dynamics of the wayward brother's return. It has not been easy for the Christian community or its official representatives to understand the Father of the parable and to distinguish reconciliation with God and his creation from juridical criminal proceedings of secular societies in our sinful history. Yet again and again the biblical inspiration breaks through to correct both the practice and the theory.

From what has been said above, it is clear that the forgiveness of God and the reconciliation of the sinner is not something that happens at a later stage in consequence of the repentance and conversion. To repent is to be forgiven; to turn is to be reconciled because the Father has been waiting only for the response that makes the outpouring of his compassion possible within the freedom of the creature which he respects and therefore will not annihilate. In other words, there is no such thing as meriting or earning forgiveness and reconciliation; one can only accept it as undeserved but unstinting mercy. Therefore, the doing of penance, the performing of works of penance, can never be seen as punitive or compensatory. It cannot have any role other than the acceptance of reconciliation as pure gift. In other words, it can only fill the function of free creaturely participation in that transformation of being, vision, relationships and actions, knowing that the transformation is a gift of grace and therefore a gift to be received in our freedom. All this the community is called to mediate or make possible by its embodiment of the compassion of God which is Christ.

Recommended Readings

Piet Schoonenberg, S.J., *Man and Sin* (Notre Dame, Ind.: Notre Dame Press, 1965).

Sean Fagan, S.M., *Has Sin Changed?* (Wilmington, Del: Michael Glazier, Inc., 1977).

Rudolf Schnackenburg, *The Moral Teaching of the New Testament* (N.Y.: Herder, 1965).

Daniel Durken, O.S.B., ed., *Sin, Salvation and the Spirit* (Collegeville: The Liturgical Press, 1979).

A powerful Jewish perspective on the question of sin and repentance is presented in:
Abraham Isaac Kook, *The Lights of Penitence* (Ramsay, N.J.: Paulist Press, 1978).

An extraordinary testimony of Christian understanding of sin and repentance from the second century is offered in:
Hermas, *The Shepherd,* which can be found in translation *e.g.* in:
Francis X. Glimm *et al.,* translators, *The Apostolic Fathers* (Washington, D.C.: Catholic University of America Press, 1947).

CHAPTER II

RITES OF PENANCE AND RECONCILIATION IN THE PATRISTIC CHURCH

The community's mediation of repentance, conversion and reconciliation is in one sense the whole task of being Church, being People of God. It is the task of the redemption still continually being accomplished by the power of the transcendent God at work in the world in the intimacy of the Holy Spirit expressed tangibly in the presence of the Risen Christ embodied in his members. This task of reconciliation, of welcome, of creative and forgiving relationships, which makes repentance and conversion possible, is diffused, subtle, sometimes elusive. It includes a very broad sweep of *anamnesis*, that is, of not forgetting, of continually drawing into consciousness much that is hard to acknowledge. It means not repressing or ignoring the suffering in which our alienation or basic sinfulness manifests itself.

That suffering ranges from the individual and private, such as boredom, frustration, anxieties, loneliness, anger, resentments, envy and sadness, through a whole labyrinth of painful experiences in inter-personal relationships such as distrust, quarrels, betrayals, dissimulations, one-up-manship games, exclusions, factions and so forth, into the vast complexity of social structures where people suffer terrible miseries from wars, poverty, famine, brutalizing working and living conditions, discrimination and contempt, political and economic injustices of all kinds and a pervasive sense of helplessness and hopelessness. All these kinds of suffering express the challenge of *anamnesis,* of becoming aware of the sinfulness of our human condition, of our state of alienation from the Father's house. The community cannot become part of the reconciliation of the world to God in Christ without being constantly attuned to the call of such suffering in all dimensions of its life experience and in all dimensions of its response as community.

However, the *anamnesis,* the "coming to oneself" or "coming to one's senses", which is the underlying condition for the community's mediation of reconciliation in which it makes repentance possible, cannot be only the remembering of suffering and the awareness of sinfulness. It must also be the remembrance of the peace and joy, the harmony and "at-homeness" of the Father's house. Reconciliation is the task of the whole community that is Church, in all its ordinary, not specifically religious activities, and it is a task poised in eschatological tension between the wonderful gift of God that already is in and among us as a foretaste of the Kingdom and the yearning and groaning of all creation for what is not yet (*cf.* Rom. 8:14-30).

The great sacrament of repentance, then, is the Church itself. The transformed and transforming community is that efficacious sign of the grace of conversion that powerfully effects what it signifies because of the way it links people and situations to the action of God in Christ Jesus. This continuing reconciliation, sacramental in a broad and true sense, is happening in people's kitchens and family rooms and bedrooms, on streets, in buses and where they shop, in offices, factories and farms, in playgrounds, theaters and hospitals, on Monday, Tuesday and the rest of the week. That is where the Church lives and breathes and plays its role in the redemption. What is done in church buildings on Sundays and special liturgical occasions gives focus and clarity and motivation to the "secular" life of the community that is Church. It does not substitute for the radical and pervasive transformation that must happen in the totality of life together in the world and in history. The Church which is the great inclusive sacrament of repentance is co-extensive with that totality of life together as it is lived by those who are the followers of Jesus.

The great central rite of repentance and reconciliation in which the community of the followers of Jesus makes its task and intention explicit is the Eucharist. From earliest times, the solemn rite of reconciliation of the Church has been the Eucharist.[1] It is an action that makes Christians participate personally and communally in the redeeming act of God in Christ Jesus. It is an act which places each local community that celebrates it at Calvary in the context of the death of Jesus, an act that invites a radical rethinking of our relation to God and to one another, an act that is the action of Jesus himself into which we are drawn to be personally and communally transformed in the totality of our lives and relations and social structures in the world. The Eucharist, as the central focus in which Church is shaped as reconciliation, is constantly repeated by the community because the whole task of repentance, conversion and reconciliation is a long, slow and gradual one for the individuals and for the community and for the world.

Although the Eucharist in its entirety is a rite of reconciliation, Christians have since earliest times found it helpful and necessary to underscore this in more explicit ways. Preeminent among these explicit ways has been the recitation of the Lord's prayer in the Eucharist.[2] This is a prayer of the community acknowledging its relationship with God as Father and is therefore at the very heart of the "turning". Moreover, its whole thrust is eschatological, that is, it is

---

[1]For a fuller explanation of this, see J.-M. Tillard, "The Bread and the Cup of Reconciliation", in *Sacramental Reconciliation*, ed. Edward Schillebeeckx (N.Y.: Herder, 1971). See also Nathan Mitchell, "Table of the Eucharist: Christian Fellowship and Christian Forgiveness" in *Rite of Penance: Commentaries. Vol. III. Background and Directions,* ed. Nathan Mitchell (Washington, D.C.: The Liturgical Conference, 1978).

[2]For indications of the role it played in the Eucharist of the early Church as a ritual of reconciliation, see Godfrey Diekmann, "Reconciliation through the Prayer of the Community" in Mitchell, ed., *op. cit.*

concerned with the final reconciliation of the world and of the human community to God. Finally, it acknowledges dependence not only of the whole community on God but of the members of the community on one another for forgiveness and reconciliation. It is not strange, therefore, that the ancient custom was not only to recite the Lord's prayer publicly and solemnly in the Eucharist but also to recite it privately three times a day. It is the prayer of Jesus himself who pleads in his members for reconciliation, that is, for repentance and forgiveness. It is a prayer, therefore, that rises in the community with the transforming power of the Spirit. Among the Church Fathers, Augustine particularly refers to the praying of the Lord's prayer by the community as the ordinary way that the daily sins of Christians are forgiven.[3]

Besides the Lord's prayer before the communion we have, of course, even today a brief rite of repentance and reconciliation at the beginning of the Eucharistic celebration. It includes an exhortation, a generic confession of sin by the assembled local community, and a prayer containing a formula of absolution said by the presiding celebrant. These special rites of repentance within the Eucharistic celebration are not an addition to the meaning and content of the Eucharist but serve to emphasize and draw out the meaning that is intrinsic to it.

While the Eucharist is the continuing central reconciliation ritual by which the Church is constituted as the body of the Risen Jesus, making the redemptive power of God present by the breathing of the Spirit in the world, there is clearly a need for another kind of conversion ritual by which an individual becomes a member of that body that is the Church. The great initial rite of repentance, conversion and reconciliation for the individual in the Church has always been baptism. Clearly, in the early centuries when baptism

---

[3]*Sermons 351 & 352* and *On Faith & Good Works*, 26. For the relevant texts of Augustine see Paul F. Palmer, *Sources of Christian Theology, Vol. II: Sacraments and Forgiveness* (Westminster, Md.: Newman, 1959), pp. 96-109.

was considered basically as the ritual, the mystery, of the initiation of adults into the community, the element of conversion and reconciliation was strong and evident to all. In the first three centuries when Christians were a frequently persecuted minority in a thoroughly pagan world, the conversion was dramatic. It involved an actual turning to God from idolatry, a turning to God in faith and trust and love from ways of life quite evidently incompatible with faith. It generally involved stark choices and sometimes heroic renunciations and risks.

Under those circumstances it is not surprising that in the first few centuries there was a general understanding that baptism was normally the only special rite of repentance that a person should need. This repentance was obviously mediated by the community that embodied the grace and presence of the Lord. To be welcomed by the community and drawn into its way of life and hope and worship was to be turned around, turned towards God, re-entering the Father's house. Once inside, the new Christian was certainly not expected to be entirely sinless, but it was understood that the life of the community of believers would continually mediate forgiveness and conversion from "daily sins" for its members by the Eucharistic celebration, by prayer together but also by the life and deeds of charity in the community. To this day, that quiet and pervasive ministry of reconciliation has not changed, though other special rituals have been added in the course of time.

Even in the era covered by the documents of the New Testament the community of the followers of Jesus had to confront the question of what to do about an individual who might totally betray the community or its way of life, thus causing a serious scandal, in the original sense of a stumbling block for others. The two canonical letters of Paul to the Corinthians suggest an improvised procedure of excommunication of the one who is a scandal to the community and to outsiders who might otherwise join the community (I Cor. 5:1-5). It is noteworthy, however, that in this passage the excommunication is clearly intended not only for the protection of the community but for the ultimate salvation of the culprit. Moreover, there is clearly also a reconciliation with the community available to those who have offended seriously enough to cause grave difficulties to the whole community (II Cor. 2: 5-11).

The question recurred constantly, of course, during the first three centuries, especially during the many times of bitter persecution. It was unfortunately but understandably not unknown for some of the weaker members of the community to betray others or the Church in various ways out of fear for themselves. If such people wanted to return to the Church after the time of persecution, the question of a second baptism or second admission was raised. The same occurred with other scandalous and public offenses. During the first three centuries such cases were the source of some dispute and finally of the custom of readmitting by a more arduous repentance or conversion than that of baptism. For the first two centuries we have no record of a standard rite by which such reconciliation was handled. However, we do know that the reconciliation was essentially readmission to the Eucharist of the local church.[4] The first indication that there was a standard ritual to be celebrated by which a person becomes an official penitent, is assigned works of

[4]See documentation from the period in translation in Palmer, *op. cit.* pp. 1-19. N.B. This excellent collection of excerpts from primary sources in translation was published in 1959. The documentation is, of course, just as useful today as then, but post-Vatican II readers would be well advised not to rely exclusively on the accompanying commentary. A safe guide to the theological interpretation is available, *e.g.* in Nathan Mitchell, ed., *op. cit.,* the editor's own essay, "Many Ways to Reconciliation: Historical Synopsis of Christian Penance" (which is, however, undocumented). See also José Ramos-Regidor, "Reconciliation in the Primitive Church and its Lessons for Theology and Pastoral Practice Today" in Schillebeeckx, ed., *op. cit.* The standard text on the history of sacramental reconciliation is still that of Bernhard Poschmann, *Penance and the Anointing of the Sick* (N.Y.: Herder, 1964). For the first three centuries see Chapters 1-3, pp. 5-80.

A very full collection of primary texts with commentary, in which Latin and Greek texts are given in the original language, Syriac, Coptic and others usually in German translation, is that of Oscar D. Watkins, *A History of Penance.* 2 vols. (London: Longmans Green and Co., 1920). Because of the nature of the work it is not outdated. Written by an Anglican scholar it is nevertheless immediately relevant to the questions that will be asked in a Roman Catholic context.

penance to do, is given the public support of the prayers of the faithful, and is finally officially reconciled with the community, seems to be in the writings of Tertullian in North Africa, reporting on the customs of the Latin speaking church there at the beginning of the third century.[5] He appears to be describing a ceremonial pattern that is already rather widely known.[6]

The rite that Tertullian describes involves the donning of penitential garb which is called "sackcloth and ashes", fasting to foster prayer, abstinence from delicacies and comfort to express sorrow, public "groaning and weeping" for sin, prostration before the presbyters of the community and kneeling before the congregation of the faithful to ask for their prayers.[7] Several points are of interest: the description is clearly not complete; it does not indicate how people become penitents nor how the process is concluded. At this stage in history it is not clear whether the bishop has a special role; it is only abundantly clear that the whole community is involved. Moreover, from other texts of Tertullian it is clear that the main preoccupation is reconciliation with the Church, for even in cases where such reconciliation is thought to be impossible, the mercy of God for a sinner is not ruled out.[8] The whole process is known by the Greek term, *exomologesis,* which is usually translated "confession". This has led some interpreters to conjecture that the process was initiated by a confession to the bishop, but this is conjecture based on later developments of reconciliation rites. More probably the "confession" involved was the whole process by which persons acknowledged themselves as sinful, in need of the help and intercession of the Church (that is the community of the faithful), and confident of the mercy of God.

---

[5]See Watkins, *op. cit., Vol. I: The Whole Church to A.D. 450.* pp. 81-92 for texts and pp. 113-128 for interpretation.

[6]*Cf. ibid.,* p. 116.

[7]*ibid.,* pp. 82-83, and *cf.* interpretation pp. 116-117.

[8]*ibid.,* pp. 81-92.

More or less contemporaneously with Tertullian, Origen does indeed speak of confession of sins, but in a context that is not the rite described by Tertullian, but seems to be envisaged as preliminary to it. Among seven biblical ways of obtaining forgiveness of sins he lists baptism, martyrdom, almsgiving, forgiveness of others, conversion of sinners, and great love. He also indicates a seventh, more arduous way, which is penance.[9] In another context,[10] Origen wrote his conviction that sins which are neither in the category he considers irremissible nor so minor that we can simply forgive one another in the context of our daily lives, may be forgiven by spiritual persons who, because they have received the Holy Spirit and manifest the fruits of the Spirit, are ministers of God in the work of remission of sins. He makes a point of it that official designation is not enough; personal holiness in the sense of authentic living by the Spirit is required. When he describes the seventh way of having sin forgiven, he writes of going to "a priest of God" to reveal one's sin and seek guidance as to whether penance (evidently the public penance or *exomologesis* of which Tertullian had written) is appropriate. Elsewhere,[11] he writes how careful one should be to find a suitable person to whom to confess one's sin, and it is by no means evident that he limits the search to priests. When he writes of the power of bishops in reconciliation of sinners, he requires that they not be sinners themselves.[12]

The Decian persecution in the middle of the third century precipitated further crises and decisions concerning the rite of reconciliation after serious sin. The principal concern was with those large numbers of Christians who apostatized or "lapsed" under threat of persecution. They fell into several

[9]*ibid.,* pp. 136-137.

[10]*De oratione,* 28. See interpretation in Watkins, *op. cit.,* p. 133.

[11]*Two Homilies on Psalm 37.* See Watkins, *op. cit.,* p. 139.

[12]*In Matthaeum,* xvi. 18. See Watkins, pp. 139-140. (N.B. Where the document is quoted in translation in the commentary, no reference is made in these footnotes to the page number for the excerpt in the original, but this can in each case be found by going to the section at the beginning of each chapter.)

categories: those who had actually sacrificed to idols and forsworn Christ, those who had fraudulently obtained certificates to that effect and were therefore safe from persecution though they had not in fact done what was described in the certificates, and those who had seriously contemplated either of the above but had not done them (possibly because their circumstances had not required immediate action). Issues were complicated by appeals to martyrs on their way to martyrdom and to confessors of the faith (who had escaped martyrdom narrowly and by chance after having faced it with the certainty of being killed) for their intercession or possibly for reconciliation itself. These issues form part of the history of the theology of the sacrament of penance which is to be discussed in Chapter 5 of this volume. However, they also gave rise to a further crystallization of the rite used to reconcile sinners. According to the testimonies we have from St. Cyprian of Carthage, there seems to have been confession to the "priest of God" (which in context meant a bishop, not any presbyter), followed by assignment and performance of appropriate penance, *exomologesis* (still meaning apparently the steps described by Tertullian), and concluded by an imposition of hands that signalled the reconciliation and allowed readmission to full participation in the Eucharist. This imposition of hands appears normally to have been the prerogative of the bishop but at least in case of deathbed reconciliations could apparently be done by a presbyter or deacon.[13]

Again, at this time, the rite is apparently used for more serious sins and for sins with public consequences. Moreover, there seems to have been no dispute over the claim that confession of Christ under persecution restores a sinner to the "peace of the Church" without any rite or formal acknowledgement of bishop or clergy or congregation. The

[13]This reconstruction, which appears to be the more reasonable one, along with the documentary evidence on which it is based, may be found in detail in Watkins, *op. cit.,* pp. 189-196. *Cf.* B. Poschmann, *op. cit.,* Ch. 3, who is however more concerned with the theology than with the shape of the rite. *Cf.* also P.F. Palmer, *op. cit.,* pp. 40-50 for translations of the key texts.

question whether the martyrs also restored others to the "peace of the Church" in a valid or legitimate sense was debated but the practice of claiming such reconciliation was an established fact of the third century. A final point of interest in this period is the repeated complaint that many who ought to be undergoing the official penance of the Church are not doing so.

Up to this time, reconciliation appears simply as readmission to full participation in the Eucharist though laying on of hands intervenes as the sign that readmission to the Eucharist is now appropriate. In the Asian churches of the latter half of the third century a more detailed pattern appears. Gregory the Wonderworker testifies to five grades or degrees of penitents, modelled on the existing pattern for the admission of catechumens but slightly more elaborate. There is no doubt that the ceremonies dramatize the readmission of the alienated to the heart of the community of worshippers.[14]

The five grades of penitents were named and defined by their relation to the liturgy. The "mourners" were those altogether outside the church who pleaded with the faithful for their prayers and for readmission. The "hearers" were those permitted to stand just within the entrance hall of the church and only during the "mass of the catechumens", that is, during the Scripture readings and homily. The "fallers" (prostrators) were allowed inside the nave of the church in a posture of self-abasement (which was apparently, however, also adopted by catechumens because baptism was also seen in the light of conversion from a life of sin). They were allowed in the nave only as long as the catechumens, that is, for the "mass of the catechumens". The "bystanders" were permitted to be present for the whole liturgy of the faithful, but were not admitted to communion. The "faithful" were those admitted to full communion.[15]

The evidence is not entirely clear, but it seems that a

---

[14]Watkins, *op. cit.*, pp. 238-246.
[15]*ibid*, p. 246.

discernment is made, probably by the bishop in person, concerning the rank or degree in which a person should be placed and concerning the length of time to be spent there. It seems also that there was a progression through these degrees culminating in full eucharistic communion, but allowing for intermediate stages of reconciliation. The document known as the *Didaskalia,* of about the same period as Gregory the Wonderworker, places heavy emphasis on the bishop's role both in the exclusion of the sinners from the Church and in the laying on of hands in reconciliation. The exclusion from the Church, that is the communion of life and worship of the Christians, is symbolized by physical exclusion from the church building where worship takes place and the Church as community of the faithful is constituted. The *Didaskalia* text seems to assume that the bishop will have no difficulty with his congregation in excluding sinners, but that he may have considerable difficulty in persuading the congregation to play their part in the reconciliation. This may have had something to do with the kind of sins for which the whole process was invoked. They were clearly sins which seriously injured the community. However, the Syriac church probably being described in the *Didaskalia* seems to know of only three degrees in the rite of exclusion and reconciliation of penitents, that is, the excluded, the penitents and the reconciled.[16]

In the early fourth century, while the western churches apparently have no really fixed pattern for penance but require in general terms that notorious sinners show works of penitence before reconciliation, some of the eastern churches have reduced the degrees of penance of Gregory Thaumatourgos to a rather rigid system. An example is a canon of the Council of Ancyra which states that those who have willingly shared in pagan sacrifices must remain "hearers" for one year, "fallers" for three and "bystanders" for two before final and full reconciliation. Other canons suggest that this six year term is a norm for offenses seen as

[16]*ibid.,* pp. 249-256.

subject to the penance of the Church. Sins that inspired particular horror in the community might be subject to as much as twenty or thirty years of official or public penance.[17] There is reference to the degrees of penance as established and normative in the proceedings of the Council of Nicea of 325.[18] In spite of this, the Church at large did not adopt the system, and indications abound that in practice after the end of the centuries of persecution, public penance was rare and increasingly dependent on the voluntary cooperation of the penitent.[19]

Part of the explanation of the declining willingness to submit to public penance or to enforce it against others is no doubt to be found in the severity of the conditions. By the end of the fourth century we have evidence from Rome that not only during the time of public penance but for the rest of one's life one had to submit to severe restrictions and disabilities.[20] In particular, the ex-penitent could not serve in the army, attend public entertainments or marry. If previously married he or she could not resume cohabitation with the spouse.

The custom had emerged at this time of reconciling penitents normally on Maundy Thursday, the Thursday before Easter. However, all are agreed that those in danger of death may be reconciled immediately if they show evident signs of penitence appropriate to their dying condition, and that this means both the imposition of hands and the offering of communion. This Maundy Thursday reconciliation ceremony was the prerogative of the bishop, but to administer the whole lengthy process of penance priest-penitentiaries had emerged. The pattern varies slightly between eastern and western churches. According to testimonies for the city

[17]*ibid.,* 273-287.

[18]Canons 11-14. See Watkins, *op. cit.,* pp. 289-292.

[19]*ibid.,* pp. 319-320.

[20]A principal source for this is a letter of Pope St. Siricius written somewhere before 398 A.D. See Watkins for text and interpretation, especially pp. 411-413. By the early fifth century the restrictions had become even more onerous and certainly more numerous. *Cf.* Watkins, p. 422.

of Rome from Pope St. Innocent I at the beginning of the fifth century, a priest (probably one of twenty-five specially appointed for this purpose) is to receive a confession from the penitent, judge the sincerity of his repentance and the adequacy of the "satisfaction", that is, of the works of penance, and declare him ready for official reconciliation by the bishop.[21]

The role of the priest-confessor in the ancient system of public penance is shown in a new light in a letter of Pope St. Leo the Great in the middle of the fifth century.[22] Leo professes himself horrified at a practice reported to him from some provinces, an illegitimate innovation in his judgment, which he roundly forbids. It seems that penitents had been required to write out an explicit account of the sins for which they were doing penance and to read this aloud at a public gathering. Leo writes that this must cease promptly, and that it is quite sufficient to confess one's sins to God and then "in secret confession" to a priest who is a suppliant on behalf of penitents. The text is of special interest because it shows that *exomologesis* did not traditionally include a public confession of specific sins. But it is also of interest because it describes the role of the priest-confessor as that of intercessor on behalf of the penitent.

This role of intercession on behalf of the penitents was not confined to the priest penitentiary. Several extant descriptions of the penitential system in Rome tell of a ceremony in which the penitents who are prostrating themselves and weeping aloud in their penitential garb are met by the bishop together with the clergy and the whole congregation, all of whom also prostrate themselves and weep aloud, identifying themselves with the penitents as one united repentant Church.[23] This was not yet the final reconciliation but the expression of solidarity of the community with the

---

[21]Watkins, *op. cit.*, pp. 415-416.

[22]*Ep. 168. Cf.* Watkins, pp. 422-424.

[23]For references and synthetic accounts of the testimonies of St. Jerome and of Sozomen see Watkins pp. 425-426.

penitents while yet they were strictly penitents. It was the intercession of the Church on their behalf to bring about their full conversion and reconciliation.

It seems that in the later period of the ancient Roman system of penance, the final reconciliation is not done by means of the imposition of hands but by a series of prayers to God which brought about reconciliation with the community at the altar and pronounced an absolution from the status of penitent.[24] In the writings of St. Ambrose of Milan it appears that such a remission in words was expressed both in the form of supplication to God and in the form of a declaration in the name of the Trinity that the sins were forgiven.[25] Yet there is an insistence that those to whom the ministry for the remission of sins is entrusted "do not exert the right of any power".

St. Augustine of Hippo, in the early fifth century, gives various indications of a penitential discipline still in effect in North Africa which agrees substantially with the foregoing.[26] It is still taken for granted that the rite of a public penance after baptism is available to a serious sinner but only once in a lifetime. Augustine lists quite specifically the traditional three categories of sins for which public penance is appropriate, namely unchastity, idolatry and homicide.[27] He refuses to answer the question whether public penance is also required for other serious sins. Augustine seems to suppose that penance is always administered by the bishop in all its phases. In other words, the private confession initiating it would be made to the bishop and the proper works of penance determined by him.[28]

With Augustine there begin to be indications of a type of

[24]The texts are known from the *Gelasian Sacramentary* (a later Gallican document) but are understood to be an earlier record of the practice of the Roman Church.

[25]*De Spiritu Sancto*, III, xviii. Quoted by Watkins, p. 433.

[26]See Watkins pp. 437-447.

[27]*De Fide et Operibus*. 19. See Watkins, p. 441.

[28]*ibid.*, p. 443.

private penance, because he seems to indicate that when a sinner confesses in secret to the bishop, the latter may assign him to do penance which would not attract public notice if this is more appropriate to the nature of the sin. This is all the more interesting as Augustine nevertheless insists that secret but serious sins ought not to be repented simply before God but also by the intervention and intercession of the Church, apparently in the person of the bishop.[29]

From the fifth century onward, the ancient discipline of public penance becomes more and more rare and attenuated. People evidently are convinced they can obtain God's forgiveness without it (which the Church Fathers and Councils and Synods had always been at pains to allow, because they would not see God's mercy as ultimately circumscribed by human restrictions). Even in the contexts in which the intervention of the Church was greatly valued, public penance was generally put off until death seemed close. Meanwhile, many people who had sinned gravely continued to communicate at the Eucharist, if the many complaints of the Church Fathers are to be believed. Indeed, some bishops such as Caesarius of Arles explicitly counseled the delay of penance, and many would not allow it to married persons except by consent of both spouses on account of the enforced life-long continence associated with it.[30]

Quite clearly, this particular rite of penance had so many disadvantages that it was not adequate as a permanent pattern for the Church through the centuries. It made a questionably sharp distinction between the sinners and the saints in the Church. It was not universally applicable (for in most churches it was not applied to clergy who sinned gravely under any circumstances). It was considered to be limited to one repentance and therefore not available to those who underwent penance early enough in life to get themselves into trouble again. Moreover, its conditions

[29]See *ibid.* for the evidence and the reconstruction of the situation. *Cf.* also R.C. Mortimer, *Origins of Private Penance in the Western Church*, (Oxford: Clarendon, 1939). Ch. IV.

[30]*Cf.* Watkins, pp. 460-465.

were so severe that many who needed it were loath to present themselves and their bishops were reluctant to urge them to it. At the same time, as a rite it has the advantage of being closely associated with the Eucharist, of involving the whole community in prayer for conversion and forgiveness of the alienated and in active participation in the process of their reconciliation with the Church, and finally also the advantage of a very dramatic enactment of the turning and the retracing of steps to the Father's house. In this sense it was very powerfully sacramental in effecting what it so clearly signified, and indeed effecting it in a way that was accessible to common experience. It seems, however, that the disadvantages were too high a price to pay for the advantages, because public penance as known to the Church of the patristic era did not survive.

However, in a treatise of John Cassian from the early fifth century there appears a first indication of another rite of penance practiced by the monks of Egypt.[31] There is no suggestion here of grave sin but of the continuing striving after a fuller Christian conversion by very devout Christians. As an integral aspect of their monastic life they are expected to reveal their thoughts and temptations as well as their deeds to an elder so as to obtain guidance in the conversion of their lives. There is no question of reconciliation with the Church because there have been no grounds for excommunication. Nevertheless, there is a certain convergence with the mild attitudes of St. John Chrysostom as patriarch of Constantinople expressed in homilies preached there about the year 400.[32] Among nine modes of penance available to sinners he lists private confession to a priest. He seems to hold this as an option in the case of serious sin and he seems to suppose not only private confession, but private penance and absolution given privately by the priest in virtue of his priestly office without further designation.

[31] *De coenobiorum institutis, Book IV.* See Watkins, p. 460.

[32] *Homilies on the Letter to the Hebrews.* Cf. Watkins, p. 478. It seems however, that Chrysostom was persecuted by fellow bishops on account of merciful positions he took.

Although it was clearly not a custom generally known among the churches, it points to a sense of freedom to create the appropriate rites for the circumstances. This practice had already been anticipated in some eastern churches by the appointment of priest-penitentiaries, because penitents reconciled by them seem at least in some cases to have enjoyed privacy in the confession, the performance of the penance and the absolution or reconciliation.[33] There is a further convergence of trends to be noted with the more flexible and more lenient and always private forms of reconciliation that were at all times extended to the dying. The way is therefore prepared for the development of a quite different and private rite of penance from the seventh century onward.

Recommended Reading

Oscar D. Watkins, *A History of Penance, being a Study of the Authorities, Vol. I: The Whole Church to A.D. 450, and Vol. II: The Western Church from A.D. 450 to A.D. 1215.* (Chapters X and XI), (London: Longmans Green & Co., 1920). While many will find these volumes too long and detailed, if they are accessible at all, most readers will appreciate the review chapters IX and XV.

The same material concerning the later patristic period in the western church is available in the following (which do not, however, include the excerpts from the primary sources):

Josef A. Jungmann, S.J., *Die Lateinischen Bussriten in ihrer geschichtlichen Entwicklung* (Innsbruck: Fel. Rauch, 1932).

---

[33]Watkins, p. 487.

Bernhard Poschmann, *Die Abendländische Kirchenbusse im Ausgang des Christlichen Altertums* (Munich: Kösel & Pustet, 1928).

A very sketchy account of the development of the rites is also available in:

Bernhard Poschmann, *Penance and the Anointing of the Sick.* (N.Y.: Herder, 1964).

The texts are available in translation in chronological order in:

Paul F. Palmer, S.J., *Sources of Christian Theology, Vol. II. Sacraments and Forgiveness* (Westminster, M.D.: Newman, 1959).

Two extraordinarily helpful sets of essays from a post-Vatican II perspective, which include historical sketches are:

Nathan Mitchell, O.S.B., ed., *The Rite of Penance: Commentaries. Vol. 3. Background and Directions.* (Washington, D.C.: The Liturgical Conference, 1978).

Edward Schillebeeckx, O.P., ed., *Sacramental Reconciliation (Concilium, Vol. 61).* (N.Y.: Herder, 1971).

CHAPTER III

GROWTH OF PRIVATE AND VOLUNTARY CONFESSION AND RECONCILIATION

Two points will be quite clear from the foregoing. First of all, though it is clear that the ministry of reconciliation in the Church dates from the commission that Jesus gave to his earliest followers, the sacrament of penance in the forms in which it has been and is celebrated in the modern Catholic Church did not exist in patristic times. Secondly, the particular rites of reconciliation were developed by the creativity and ingenuity of the community in response to the changing needs of the times, and by the end of the patristic era it was quite clear that the rite of public ecclesiastical penance was inadequate and in most situations unsuitable.

One might even say there is a certain inevitability to what happened. That is to say, that by the basic premises of Christian faith, a rite was needed which did not sharply distinguish between the sinners and the saints but acknowledged the ongoing need of conversion for all, a rite moreover which was repeatable, easy of access for all, not implying any excommunication from the body of the faithful or the Eucharistic table, but offering guidance in the living of the Christian life. As already noted, there were some tentative moves in this direction with the priest-penitentiaries, but encounters with them in a penitential rite still seemed to assume a situation of very grave sin.[1] It was, therefore, mainly from the monastic tradition that a more universal form of sacramental penance began to develop.

The history of monasticism is diffuse, but it is clear that the whole monastic movement is founded upon a vivid awareness of the pervasiveness of sin, that is, of original sin and the consequent state of disorientation of human life and society. Of course, baptism and the life of the Church as community of believers are intended as the Spirit-filled response to the sinful situation. However, because Church as it ought to be never really or fully happens, monasticism emerges in history as a kind of contingency plan for the general failure of Christian society really to be Church. Monastic profession emerges as a kind of reiteration of baptism (which is what the ancient rites of penance were also constructed to be). In other words, monastic life can be seen as an entry into a state of penitence, an entry into a rank of penitents, though without the implication that there has been the commission of grave personal sin. It is enough to be caught in the prevailing disorientation and to know oneself, therefore, as sinful and inclined to sin and called to a turning to retrace one's steps to the Father's house, that is, to reconciliation at the deepest levels of existence and of consciousness.[2] All monastic life is therefore a kind of *exomologesis.*

This clearly envisages a life-long task, one which involves difficult discernments to be made, which calls for guidance.

---

[1]Some tenuous evidence points to the origin of a system of private or non-canonical penance in the reconciliation of clerics and from the sixth century onward in deathbed reconciliations in which there might have been no grave sin to repent. The evidence, which is inconclusive, is carefully sifted in R.C. Mortimer, *The Origins of Private Penance in the Western Church* (Oxford: Clarendon, 1939). Mortimer gives special attention to the theories of Galtier and others concerning the existence of private penance from the earliest times, which are not discussed in this volume.

[2]The account here given of the role of confession and repentance in monasticism is based upon H. Dörries, "The Place of Confession in Ancient Monasticism", (transl. from the German by Hans Frei), in *Studia Patristica*, Vol. V, ed. F.L. Cross, collected in *Texte u. Untersuchungen, Band 80.* (Berlin: Akademie Verlag, 1962), pp. 284-309.

This is the basis of the quest for an elder, a trustworthy, tried and tested holy person, as a spiritual father or mother. When one has found such, one opens all the secrets of one's heart and mind. This is not a confession of sins only, but a "manifestation of conscience", that is, a disclosure of one's thoughts and feelings, fears and hopes, loathing and striving temptations and inspirations. In fact it seems often to have been concerned with obtaining guidance in distinguishing what are temptations and what are divine inspirations. "...The one to whom one turns assumes a parental role in which understanding and ability to help are based on affection and on seniority not only in age but in spiritual maturity, providing a model of what the spiritual child hopes to be. For this reason it is not any other ascetic who can be chosen as spiritual guide, nor can one ever arrogate the task to oneself."[3]

In the tradition of the desert ascetics an interesting tension develops. Because it is so necessary to reveal one's inner life in order truly to experience the grace of God as liberating one's authentic self and to experience the shadow or darkness of all that is inauthentic and disoriented in one's life and personal experience, it is a work of great compassion and constructive charity for the spiritual guide to elicit confession from younger monks.[3] Yet this is not done by any sort of cross-questioning or bullying or imposition of rules, but rather by warm, compassionate presence and by humble personal testimony on the part of the spiritual elder. There is no element of judgement of the person, only of discernment of the movement of the Spirit in that person's conversion (for all alike are seen as sinners) and of discernment of the remedies for what is not well. There is also an implicit sacramental theology in the desert practice of confession, because there is a strong conviction that the counsel given by such a guide in such a context is a special charismatic

---

[3]Dörries, *op. cit.*, p. 288 ff. For evidence of the fact that these traditions applied to women of the desert as well as men, see Helen Waddell, *The Desert Fathers* (Ann Arbor, MI; University of Michigan Press, 1957).

word. To obey it is unfailingly to be on the road to salvation.[4]

The real tension, however, arises when a monk transgresses gravely in such a way as to threaten the quest for perfection by others. Stories abound of councils called on the pattern of the Church's official discipline of public penance, at which some of the fellow monks have planned to call the erring one to account and impose severe penance on him as a condition for subsequent reconciliation with the fellowship of the desert monks. In all of these stories an older and holier monk breaks up the proceedings by a symbolic gesture in which he places himself in the same category as the culprit and claims that the same penalty must then be imposed upon him as upon the accused.[5] The whole tradition of the desert was brought into what was in effect a sharp critique of the ancient Church discipline of public penance.

Out of their own experience of desert life in quest of Christian perfection, the monks resisted the division of a Christian community into saints and sinners, therefore they resisted the notion of excommunication as punishment. They did favor a three day period of repentance as a kind of retreat of more intense recollection, which was apparently ended with an *agape* or fellowship meal with other monks.[6] The three days' penitence are not intended for the penitent's punishment or his expiation of guilt but for his healing by greater awareness of what has happened in his sinning and greater awareness of the grace and call of God. The issue is not only that according to the desert tradition the elders have become aware of universal sinfulness and therefore do not want to judge others, though this too is frequently asserted, but beyond this they are convinced that particular sinful actions are symptomatic of the sinfulness that is much deeper and more pervasive so that sin can never be expiated.

[4]Dörries, *op. cit.*, p. 289.

[5]*ibid.*, p. 291 ff. See especially stories on p. 295 ff.

[6]*ibid.*, pp. 291-292.

Expiation is for the desert fathers simply an incorrect category applied to the problem. The proper category is that of healing. The healing is the gift of God and all that can be done in repentance is to lay oneself open to the grace of God working in one's life and in one's innermost depths. The monks are, as evidenced by many desert stories, not averse to doing this (that is, laying themselves open to God's grace) by severe fasting, vigils and lonely watching, lives of utter austerity and hardship and frightening simplicity, all of which would seem to us today to constitute rather rigorous penance. But there is a slow, patient quality in the way they do it; anything that has an air of the frantic or the desperate is gently reproved by the elders because it does not open the individual to the grace of God which is the real healing force.

As though to underscore the several points just mentioned, the stories of the desert fathers give a further hint. When an older monk by his humility and compassion has induced another to confess serious sin, he persuades him to undertake a more rigorous fast to open his life to the healing power of God but he also promises to lighten the burden by undertaking the same fast himself and he intercedes passionately with God on behalf of his penitent.[7]

The tradition of such confessions and such practices of repentance carried over into the monasteries of Europe. Thus, for instance, the Rule of St. Benedict speaks of a ladder of humility and discipline by which one must climb to reach the heavenly heights. "The fifth step of humility is achieved when a monk, by humble confession, discloses to his abbot all the evil thoughts in his heart and evil acts he has carried out. The Scripture tells us to do this ... "[8] There follows a string of biblical quotations which alleviates a little the otherwise totally negative impression of what happens in the manifestation of conscience to the abbot. It is further alle-

---

[7]From testimonies concerning Abba Lot, *ibid.,* p. 290.

[8]*The Rule of St. Benedict*, ed. Timothy Fry, O.S.B. (Collegeville, MN: Liturgical Press, 1981), Ch. 7.

viated by the later observation that "when a monk has climbed all twelve steps, he will find that perfect love of God which casts out fear, by means of which everything he had observed anxiously before will now appear simple and natural".[9]

However, the monasteries are not able to follow the reluctance of the desert fathers in assigning blame or punishment to others. Probably out of sheer necessity to maintain order and peace in large establishments, they have strict disciplinary codes. The Rule of St. Benedict provides that transgressors shall be admonished by their superiors twice in private and then, if they have not "made amends", once in public, after which, failing any change, they are to be "excommunicated" and if this also is unsuccessful are to undergo corporal punishment.[10] The excommunication referred to here is not expulsion from the monastery but from the fellowship at meals and in common worship and work.[11] Explicitly the case is stated that the abbot must have compassion and deep concern to win offenders back but that ultimately if there is no repentance and conversion there must be explusion from the monastery so that one recalcitrant brother does not "infect" others and harm the community.[12] This seems to bring the tradition almost full circle back to the discipline of public penance in the Church, though it is to be noted that even the expelled may be allowed back into the monastery in full (though penitential) reconciliation twice, in contrast to the once only canonical penance of the Church.[13] Indeed the custom that arose in the

[9]*ibid. Cf.* also the more positive light on the relationship with the abbot in Ch. 49 on voluntary observances of Lent.

[10]*ibid.*, Ch. 23.

[11]*ibid.*, Chs. 24 & 25.

[12]*ibid.*, Chs. 27 & 28.

[13]*ibid.*, Ch. 29. For a more benign interpretation of the relationship between the tradition of the desert fathers and that of the monasteries of the western church, see Raymond Studzinski, OSB, "The Minister of Reconciliation: Some Historical Models", in *Rite of Penance: Commentaries, Vol. III, Background and Directions,* ed. Nathan Mitchell, OSB. (Washington, D.C.: Liturgical Conference, 1978).

western Church of allowing repentant and even notorious sinners to go to a monastery as *conversi* (penitent associates) instead of doing an assigned period of public penitence seems to be a tacit admission that the monasteries were doing the same thing better.

The relation of the monastically excommunicated to the common worship of the community in choir is parallel to that of the penitents in public canonical penance. They are to prostrate themselves at the oratory door as the Divine Office is ending and lie there in silence as the brothers pass. When the abbot allows them to enter the oratory (apparently a second stage towards reconciliation), they are to throw themselves at the feet of the abbot and then of the brothers that they may pray for them. When the abbot gives the signal for the next step they may take their places in the choir but may not yet chant, read or participate actively, but must at the end of each "hour" of the Divine Office prostrate themselves like the "fallers" of the eastern degrees of penance. A final blessing of the abbot eventually ends the "punishment" (which is so designated in the Rule).[14]

Apart from the experience of the *conversi*, it is in the Celtic and British churches that the monastic tradition of penance begins to affect the Christian community at large. A Welsh testimony dating from the sixth century, possibly a little later than the Rule of St. Benedict, gives a tariff system of penances for various offenses in a context which describes a system of private penance involving reconciliation with the Church and renewed access to the Eucharist. It is not administered by the bishop at any stage, does not involve public acts of penance or an official status of penitent in the Church, and does not involve any rite of reconciliation other than readmission to Eucharistic communion.[15]

---

[14]*Rule of St. Benedict*, Ch. 44 *Cf*, however, admonitions to the abbot in Ch. 64 which reminds him of his own frailty and of the discretion and compassion he should have in balancing the need for conversion with human weakness.

[15]Oscar D. Watkins, *A History of Penance. Vol. II. The Western Church from A.D. 450 to A.D. 1215.* (London: Longmans Green & Co., 1920), pp. 603-604. *N.B.* For almost all references to this work given in this chapter, shorter excerpts

Confession, apparently to the abbot of a monastery, is implied by the description. This penance seems to apply to monks and to other persons connected with the monastery in some way. However, the tariff of penance lists sins for which canonical penance was traditionally required, and it is evident that such reconciliation with the Church is understood by the readmission to Eucharistic communion. Therefore it clearly substitutes for canonical or public penance under the auspices of the bishop.

Later documents of the British churches seem to indicate a more or less spontaneous extension of such penance to other Christians.[16] The Welsh churches (which meant basically monasteries and their spheres of influence) sent at least one mission to the Irish church in the mid sixth century to restore the fervor and discipline which that church had been losing since the days of St. Patrick.[17] Out of this influence came several manuals or "penitentials" which deal with penance under the authority of abbots by a wide variety of people, large numbers of students studying at the monastery (at least some of whom were clerics), others who seem to have presented themselves at the monastery for advice or as voluntary penitents, and certainly women as well as men. The abbots functioned independently of any bishop in the penance and reconciliation of these people.

There is a tariff of penances, comparable with the canonical penance of the ancient Church, by both the time and the severity of the penance imposed. The tariff, however, allows some discretion on the part of the abbot. Confession is presupposed, the penance does not involve penitential garb or public humiliation, or admission to a rank of penitents. It usually involves a fast of greater or lesser severity. The penitent cannot be "restored to the altar", that is, readmit-

from the primary sources are also available in translation in Paul F. Palmer, *Sources of Christian Theology. Vol. II. Sacraments and Forgiveness.* (Westminster, Md.: Newman Press, 1959).

[16]*E.g.,* Synods of St. David and Excerpts from the *Book of David. Cf.* Watkins, *op. cit.,* Vol. II, pp. 605-606.

[17]*ibid.,* p. 606.

ted to eucharistic communion, until the penance is completed, but when it is completed there is no special ceremony
involved in the reconciliation and the bishop is not involved.
In the Penitential of Finian in the second half of the sixth
century, it appears that priests are not usually involved
either.[18] It is the holiness of the monks, and particularly of
the abbots, that inspires people to go to them voluntarily to
seek penance and conversion and leads people to have
confidence that their mediation of reconciliation is effective
with God and His Church. Moreover, the social, educa-
tional and administrative functions of the monasteries seem
to require that reconciliations be handled by them.

The penitential of Columbanus, a little later than that of
Finian, describes penance and reconciliation for all kinds of
people and a wide range of offenses. When dealing with
people who evidently are not inmates of the monastery, it
prescribes the penance to be performed and specifies that
only upon completion may the penitent "be joined to the
altar by the sentence of the priest".[19] This seems to refer to
readmission to full participation in the Eucharist. There is
no other reference to a rite of reconciliation, but the authority of the priest is instrumental in the restoration to eucharistic communion even though the penance has been done
under monastic guidance, presumably after confession to an
abbot or monk. The penances prescribed appear to be in the
monastic tradition, such as fasting on bread and water or
abstaining from certain foods, exile for a prescribed period
where public scandal was involved, renunciation of goods
and shorter or longer periods in a monastery.

According to the evidence offered us by Columbanus,
who compiled his penitential not for the British Isles but for
Gaul where he had founded monasteries, there was at this
time in the later sixth century still a custom of public
penance and public reconciliation by the bishop in person in
the case of heretics. The custom appears even at this time,

[18]*ibid.,* pp. 606-612.
[19]See examples in Watkins, p. 617.

however, as rather strange because the instructions for implementing it are awkward and seem to assume that readers will have difficulty understanding them.[20]

At the same time, and especially from the seventh century onwards, there begin to be testimonies that frequent voluntary, devotional confession of minor faults is being encouraged not only in monasteries but for others. There is no mention of any absolution in the modern sense nor of any reconciliation ritual in the sense of the ancient canonical penance. It seems to be simply an extension of the desert and monastic custom of manifestation of conscience in order to obtain guidance and help in a continuing conversion of one's life. How little this was associated with priesthood is clear from the indications that such confessions were also made to women. Thus in the Celtic tradition it is alleged that Columbanus himself for a period of his life used to make his confession to a woman, and that both Brigit and Ita of Cluain Credill served as confessors.[21] Outside the Celtic tradition it is evidenced by an instruction given by St. Donatus to nuns.[22]

Even in the seventh century there is evidence that bishops trained in the monastic tradition or influenced by it, while required to hold a public reconciliation ceremony on Holy Thursday, are implicitly or explicitly approving a system of private penance administered apparently either by priests or by non-ordained monks. This appears in the context of a pervasive conviction that confession of sins, performance of prescribed penance and reconciliation are useful to all Christians and not only in exceptional cases. This is certainly so in the church of Gaul,[23] while in England, as is well known, there is no evidence that the Roman or ancient

[20]*ibid.*, p. 617-618.

[21]This assertion is frequently made but without documentation, *e.g.* by Kenneth Leech in *Soul Friend: A Study in Spirituality* (London: Sheldon Press, 1977), p. 50.

[22]Watkins, *op. cit.*, p. 621.

[23]For evidence, see *ibid.*, pp. 625-627, and corresponding excerpts from primary sources in Watkins or Palmer.

system of public, canonical penance had ever been in use. The whole English church had adopted the Celtic system with its private and repeatable penance.[24]

From penitentials, or manuals for priest-confessors around the end of the seventh and beginning of the eighth centuries, we can form some general impression of what this early private penance was like.[25] It was administered by a priest or a bishop but apparently in cases of necessity also by a deacon. When a penitent comes to the priest (for it would more usually be a priest), the latter is first to withdraw briefly to pray. A text for the prayer is given. In it the priest humbly acknowledges before God that he himself is a sinner chosen in spite of his utter unworthiness to intercede with the Lord Jesus Christ for others in their repentance. The rest of the prayer consists of such intercession. His own sorrow for sin is to be as evident as possible to the aspiring penitent.

When penitent and priest meet there is a confession of sin and the priest is to judge whether the penitent is in earnest. If he is he must be received and given counsel. A fast is to be assigned immediately, of which both the length and the conditions are to be specified. This is all to be clarified to spare the penitent the mortification of having to go through the confession a second time later to determine conditions more exactly. The fast may be more or less stringent and may be for as long as ten years. However, Saturdays and Sundays are free days. The length and the type of fasting is to be determined by the general rules laid down in the penitential, but the priest is to judge whether the penitent is able to sustain such a fast. He is to be particularly lenient with "servants", that is, presumably, with people who are poor and do heavy manual labor. He has the possibility of commuting the whole fast for a money payment according to the means of the penitent. Such money is to be given for the redemption of captives, the relief of the poor or "left on

---

[24]Watkins, *op. cit.,* pp. 643-644.

[25]*ibid.,* pp. 628-630. The relevant texts of the so-called *Roman Penitential* for the church of Gaul at this time are given in full in Latin on pp. 598-601.

the altar", presumably for the upkeep of the church.

A particularly interesting point is that whenever a fast is imposed, the priest himself is to share it with the penitent for one or two weeks or as long as he can so that he may not come under Jesus' condemnation of those who place insupportable burdens on men's shoulders and fail to move a finger of their own to lift them.[26] At the same time there is a caution against too lightly exonerating those who can fast, because it is "a debt", that is, the performance of the fast is seen as a purification from sin because there is a danger of the sinner's returning to the former habit or sin. Indeed penitents are to be encouraged to fast voluntarily beyond the assigned penance because they will be rewarded and gain the kingdom of heaven.[27]

A number of Psalms and prayers are specified to be said by the priest. The reconciliation at the end of the penance is effected by a laying on of hands. There is an accompanying prayer of petition offered to God, the Father Almighty, through Jesus Christ. It addresses God who by Jesus Christ has "deigned to heal our wounds". It specifies that "we your lowly priests humbly (or pleadingly) beg and beseech you that by our prayers you deign to turn to us the ear of your loving kindness and remit all the crimes and sins. . ." The prayer does not claim to forgive sin in the name of God, but begs God to do so.[28]

There are many compassionate elements in this rite as shown us in the *pseudo-Roman Penitential*. There is the privacy, the acknowledgement that the reconciling priest is himself a sinner, the sharing of the fast by the priest, the consideration of what the penitent is able to do, the concern not to humiliate the penitent by a double confession, the sense that the purpose of the penance is to effect the turning to God from sin in an enduring way, not to punish, and the assurance of the welcoming mercy of God. All of this is

[26]Exact Latin text is given in Watkins, p. 598.

[27]*ibid.*, p. 599.

[28]*ibid.*, p. 600.

certainly in the tradition that springs from the spiritual experience and insights of the desert fathers. Yet the tariff of penances, and the very lengthy periods assigned bespeak a very different understanding of the power of God at work in human hearts in a sinful history. They make a distinction, or so it seems, between less sinful and more sinful based on particular acts in which sinfulness is manifest, and they claim to possess a measure of conversion in terms of duration and severity of hardships undergone. The Desert Fathers, on the other hand, saw no reason why God could not effect a profound conversion in the most wayward heart given three days of keen awareness of sin in intensified prayer and deep solitude. This was evidently not intended as a shortening of "the debt" of penance but as a refusal of any pretension to be able to measure penance.

In all of the foregoing there appears to be the assumption that penitents are people who have spontaneously become aware of sin in their lives, more evidently of sins, that is of discrete sinful actions. There does not seem to be any urging of people to examine their conscience with some sort of scheduled regularity and, so to speak, search for sins that might be lurking there. Yet there are two other contemporary developments that seemed to be moving in this direction. One was the way in which Lenten observance was taking shape. The other was the apparently unique Spanish rite of the Good Friday ceremony called *indulgentia*.

Lent was observed as a time of fasting in the time of St. Gregory who writes of it in his *Homilies on the Gospels* as a tithe of the year which one renders to God. Fasting had, of course, been seen since biblical times not only as a specific act of repentance, but also as a way of prayer or intensified attention to God. Gregory speaks of the Lenten fast as a tithe because in his day it had 36 fast days, beginning six weeks before Easter and omitting all the Sundays.[29] We know that this was still so in the time of St. Isidore of Seville who died about the year 636 A.D. Isidore speaks of the need

---

[29]Cited and explained in Watkins, p. 572.

of all Christians to confess to God and repent the daily sins of human frailty, but he does not seem to connect this particularly with Lent.[30] That connection first appears in the middle of the seventh century in the Holy Thursday homilies of St. Eligius of Noyon. He addresses first the whole congregation and then the public penitents separately, noting that all have need of repentance. He speaks of their having exercised themselves in penitence in the observances of the forty days.[31]

A late section of the *Gelasian Sacramentary*, as well as a collection of canons from about the mid seventh century, establish the Wednesday of the beginning of Lent as a day for the reception of penitents and the initiation of the penitential season that is to end on the Thursday of the Lord's Supper. The ceremony includes a sprinkling with holy water, imposition of haircloth, placing of ashes on the heads of the penitents and their solemn exclusion from the church for the duration of Lent. The congregation joins in the praying of the penitential psalms and other prayers for the penitents, but the whole congregation is not yet included in the ranks of the penitents. Only the official penitents receive the ashes at this stage.[32] By the late eighth century there is mention of confession to priests at the beginning of Lent, which is placed at Ash Wednesday. It is in a context in which three possible ways of repentance are recognized: public penance, private penance after confession to a priest, or private repentance with confession to God alone. Therefore it is clear that Lent as a season of penitence now applies not only to the public penitents.[33]

From the beginning of the tenth century we have testimony of an exhortation first to those "affected by a wound or mortal sin" and then to all others to confess to the priest (apparently assumed to be the parish priest) at the beginning

[30]*ibid.*, pp. 572-574.

[31]*ibid.*, pp. 577-578 and corresponding excerpts from primary sources.

[32]*ibid.*, pp. 580-581.

[33]From the *Capitularies* of Theodulf. See Watkins, pp. 694-696.

of Lent. The purpose appears to be not only to inspire repentance but to determine the appropriate works of penance to be performed by each of the faithful during that Lent.[34] It seems that by the eleventh century the devotional custom of receiving ashes as a token of entering Lent as a voluntary penitent was widespread, and this custom has endured to the present.[35]

A custom which did not spread, but which seems to have had the same motivation was that of the rite of *indulgentia* in the Mozarabic liturgy of Spain.[36] In the late sixth and early seventh centuries in Spain the discipline of allowing only one public and canonical penance and reconciliation was strictly enforced. Yet the sense of universal sinfulness and actual sinning was evidently also strong. The *Mozarabic Breviary* gives us an account of a rite which it seems the Fourth Council of Toledo in 633 A.D. made obligatory. It takes place on Good Friday. All the people are gathered in the church and are instructed to "pray as penitents", kneeling, to beg forgiveness of their sins. There are instructions several times to rise or to kneel and finally to fall prostrate. *"Indulgentiam"* is chanted three hundred times at the end of a first series of prayers which constitute a generic confession of sin by the whole congregation. It is chanted two hundred times at the end of a second series of prayers and one hundred times at the end of a third.

Although it is not possible to reconstruct the rite in full, and although there are actually two variant forms of it in the documentary testimonies, [37] it clearly constitutes a reconciliation ritual under the official auspices of the Church, admitting those who took part in it with sincere repentance

---

[34] From the compilation of canons by Regino of Prüm. See Watkins, pp. 713-714.

[35] *Cf.* Josef Jungmann, *Die lateinischen Bussriten in ihrer geschichtlichen Entwicklung* (Innsbruck: Fel. Rauch, 1932), pp. 59 ff. Actually, at the end of the century it was even made mandatory, as here documented by Jungmann, but this did not endure.

[36] Described and analyzed in detail in Watkins, *op. cit.*, pp. 585-587. See extensive excerpts from the Latin texts in *ibid.*, p. 533.

[37] *ibid.*, text pp. 534-535, commentary pp. 585-586.

to eucharistic communion at Easter, and repeatable every year. There appears to be in the injunctions of the Fourth Council of Toledo a tacit admission that the rite is being used by those guilty of serious sin and that no further confession or penance is required of them than the generic confession made aloud by the whole congregation and the specific confession of one's sins made silently to God alone. No distinction is being made, therefore, between a category of "sinners" and a category of the "faithful" in this rite. Moreover, there is no imposition of a lengthy penance, though the prayers seem to assume that the Lenten fast has been observed, and because there is no confession to a priest participants are left as judges of the sincerity of their own repentance as the condition for the Easter communion.

What we know of the rite is in many ways reminiscent of the Yom Kippur services of the Jewish community — a very long time spent in church, a service that is calculated to elicit affective as well as intellectual acknowledgement of sinfulness, a long and passionate pleading for forgiveness and reconciliation quite dramatically expressed by the whole congregation acting and crying out as one, and the annual repetition. Many elements of this rite, especially in the varient form[38], have survived into the Good Friday services of our own time, though without the understanding that it serves as ecclesiastical reconciliation of grave sinners, admitting them to eucharistic communion at Easter.

[38]See footnote 37.

Recommended Reading

See bibliography for Chapter II. Further relevant books are:

Kenneth Leech, *Soul Friend: A Study of Spirituality.* (London: Sheldon, 1977).

Paul Anciaux, *The Sacrament of Penance.* (N.Y.: Sheed & Ward, 1962).

R.C. Mortimer, *The Origins of Private Penance in the Western Church.* (Oxford: Clarendon, 1939).

Helpful on the history of penitential rituals involving the whole congregation, such as Lent, Advent, Ember days and Rogation days (a history that is not set out in detail in this volume) is:

Francis X. Weiser, S.J., *Handbook of Christian Feasts and Seasons.* (N.Y.: Harcourt, Brace & World, 1958).

CHAPTER IV

MERGER OF TRADITIONS AND CONSEQUENT PROBLEMS

The last two chapters have described in some detail the sources from which our post-baptismal penitential rites developed in the early centuries of Christian history. What we have had since the later Middle Ages resulted from a practical and theoretical merger of the two major strands of these traditions. This has also left unresolved problems. One point is quite clear from the history: the community has in the past developed the rites according to the needs of the times, therefore it can assuredly continue to do this in the present and future.

Before looking at the merger of the traditions historically, it will be useful to look at the two main types of penance in terms of their respective functions and goals. The ancient rite of public or canonical penance was seen as a "second plank" in case of post-baptismal shipwreck. It was a rescue operation devised for an abnormal situation. It was something of a scandal within the Church that this rescue operation was needed at all, so much so that in most local churches through most of the patristic era it was allowed only once to any individual. It envisaged behavior that gravely damaged the community of believers as well as the one who had sinned. It was built basically around the need to exclude, that is ex-communicate, such a one and the persistent realization that it was more in the spirit of Jesus and according to the boundless mercy of God to make a re-entry to the community possible. It was also based on an understanding, at first tacit and later explicit, that baptism could not be repeated.

Necessarily, therefore, a basic preoccupation of the Church and its responsible representatives in the administration of the ancient discipline of canonical penance was the determination of the conditions for readmission. The relationship of the degrees of penance to the Eucharist and the physical pattern of readmission to the church building for community worship dramatized this aspect. The determination of the conditions, both in general and in the particulars for each penitent, had to be made with several factors in mind. A prime consideration was the building and maintaining of the Christian community as the kind of presence of the Risen Christ in the world which it was called to be. On the one hand it was called to be a community of the redeemed, of those who had tasted the coming of the Reign of God, of those who lived by the Spirit in holiness of life, an efficacious and strikingly evident sign of salvation present in history. On the other hand the community of believers was called to pilgrimage in the course of an historical struggle in a sinful world, in which the Church itself remains full of ambivalence and ambiguity and none is past temptation. Fraternal charity and deep communion in the struggle and aspiration is at the very heart of the redemption. So is practical compassion expressed in spiritual as well as corporal ways of expressing mercy. There is a necessary tension here between the "already" of the holiness of the Church founded upon Jesus and living by his Spirit in response to the Father's call and the "not yet" of the continuing struggle to realize this fully in all the members and in all facets of its life in the world. Thus there is the conflict between the scandal of patently unholy members and the scandal of an ultimately unmerciful community.

The second major consideration in setting the terms for readmission to, or reconciliation with, the community was the question concerning the sinning individual and the most effective ways of guiding that individual into a new, that is post-baptismal, and far-reaching repentance with strong promise of life-long perseverance. Much of the public humiliation, onerous works of repentance, highly dramatized exclusions, exorcisms, and prayers with tears and prostrations, as well as the solemnity of the return to the bosom of the community and to the eucharistic communion, was certainly intended to bring the penitent to such dispositions as would open the way for the grace of a deeper faith, trust and commitment than those that had proved inadequate to the temptations of life before. In terms, then, not only of the impact on the community but also of the situation of the sinning individual, the canonical penance customs sprang from a sense of acute crisis calling for dire emergency measures.

A crucial determination that had obviously to be made in this context was that of the specific sins which called for such drastic measures. Throughout the patristic era there appears to have been general agreement that apostasy, homicide and unchastity were the principal "capital sins" that so damaged the community and the individual that they called for the remedy of canonical penance.[1] This was unsatisfactory in several ways. It left some appalling gaps such as plundering and pillaging and torturing. It never satisfactorily settled the question of secret sins, such as homicides and adulteries not known to the Christian community but presumably nevertheless corrupting its fabric from within. Moreover it left the content of the capital sins rather ill-defined, as in the cases where planned homicides and adulteries were frustrated and never actually executed, or when apostasy in time of persecution was contemplated and turned out not to be necessary to escape arrest. Eventually, there came to be an uncomfortable awareness that there was something unhealthily self-righteous about this category of

---

[1]Most of the witnesses do not limit public penance to these categories, but neither do they specify any other categories. *Cf.* Bernard Poschmann, *Penance and the Anointing of the Sick* (N.Y.: Herder, 1964), p. 84 ff.

capital sins which put those sinners and not others into a position of public ignominy and condemnation.

This unease led to the avoidance of canonical penance by those theoretically liable to it, simultaneously with its adoption on their deathbeds by those theoretically not liable at all. Thus it is known of Isidore of Seville that, though certainly not claiming to be guilty of any capital sins and though theoretically not even eligible for canonical penance because he was a bishop, he nevertheless insisted on undergoing the shortened version of public penance on his deathbed, in the same pattern as the most notorious criminal.[2] Even short of these more dramatic manifestations, the developments traced in the previous chapter concerning Lent and the Indulgentia in Spain point in the same direction — the disappearance of the separate category of public penitents and the assimilation of the whole community into the stance of the penitents. Although the practice of excommunication has never been completely abandoned, it came to be limited to exclusion from eucharistic communion and even that is, in our own time, practically dependent upon the voluntary submission and cooperation of the excluded except in the most conspicuous and notorious cases.

The ancient practice was too harsh and too inauthentic in the light of the gospel and could not endure. Yet it had some features whose subsequent loss left the Church significantly poorer. The most obvious of these was the clear acknowledgement of the ecclesial dimensions of sin and repentance. To sin is always to damage the fabric of the community and cause rifts that call for reconciliations within the community. Moreover the sin of each is the responsibility of all. The work of repentance and reconciliation is the work of the whole community. All must pray and mourn and fast for the sins that break the fabric of the community and all must mediate the possibilities of repentance and conversion for one another. This sense of corporate involvement tended to

---

[2]This in spite of the fact that Isidore himself records that priests and deacons (including *a fortiori* bishops) do not enter the ranks of the penitents. *Cf.* Watkins, pp. 573-574.

disappear with the gradual disuse of canonical penance, though there are remnants of its survival in the celebration of Lent, Advent, Ember and Rogation days.[3]

The monastic, Celtic, British rite of private penance is in origin in many ways the antithesis of the ancient canonical penance. It begins as a voluntary manifestation of conscience on the part of those striving more earnestly for the perfection or fullness of the Christian life. It does not involve an excommunication and therefore there is no question of any absolution from bond or interdict. For this reason, also, there is no need of an authoritative judgment on behalf of the Church, so that the authority of the bishop and his delegation of that authority to priests in certain circumstances simply does not come in question. Moreover, the custom arises in the first place among hermits and monks and is extended by them first to those connected in regular fashion with their monasteries and later to others who come to them in quest of conversion and guidance. Consequently, those who serve in this ministry that has arisen so spontaneously in the Church are monks, that is, people living a life of voluntary penitence in the quest for perfection. Their holiness and their personal experience in the pathways of penitence render them the obvious experts, and this is as true of women as it is of men leading a monastic life.

Deep in the monastic tradition as it grows from its roots among the desert hermits is the awareness of universal sinfulness and the unwillingness to judge and condemn. The conceptual model underlying the monastic understanding of penance is not that of guilt and expiation but that of woundedness and healing. The task, therefore, of the monastic confessor is not that of judging and imposing sentence of penalties but that of compassionate discernment of remedies. Moreover, the confessor does not do this in a dispassionate and detached way, but enters into passionate

---

[3]On the meaning historically given to all these, see F.X. Weiser, *Handbook of Christian Feasts and Customs* (N.Y.: Harcourt, Brace & World, 1952).

pleading with God on behalf of the penitent and with the penitent.

In the Celtic and English experience, however, something of this conviction and spirit is lost, as evidenced by the manuals known as penitentials. All kinds of people were assimilated into the monastic establishments, some of whom were not especially concerned with the pursuit of Christian perfection but were there rather in pursuit of the only available education or simply in pursuit of a livelihood. Moreover, in the monastic missionary churches, bishops whose own lives, training and commitment were those of monks, exercised a pastoral ministry caring for general congregations. It was natural enough that in Wales, Ireland and England those local churches would be administered by an extension of the monastic pattern. Yet it was likewise not surprising that the more usual penance under these circumstances began to look less like the manifestation of conscience and spiritual direction of the fervent monk and to look more like the scandalous situation of the recalcitrant monk who according to the Rule of St. Benedict had to be excommunicated from choir and table and treated harshly to be brought to the realization of his perilous condition.

Private penance administered according to the penitentials, therefore, was already a compromise. It avoided the extremes of notoriety, inaccessibility, life-long disabilities and consequent postponement to the deathbed, and most significantly of all, perhaps, it eliminated the harsh rule of only one penance. Yet it implied rather harsh judgments that certain sins could only be repented over a very long period of time. In fact the practice of the penitentials seemed to imply that the gravity of sin and the repentance from sin could be measured. So heavy was the emphasis on measurement and on comparative severity of penances that the issue had in practice become one of punishment and expiation rather than one of implementing or realizing the turning back to God in the transformation of external dimensions of life expressing the inner conversion of heart. Moreover, the actual severity of the penances listed represents a complete abandonment of the desert hermits' luminous confidence that the all-powerful mercy of God could win back the most wayward heart if given a few days of intense prayer in deep solitude.

It may be useless to speculate further why this happened. The whole history of the Church is certainly not exempt from the general human tendency to lose the fervor and purity of the beginnings of any project with the passage of time. Yet it seems to be more than accidental that the rapid spread of private penance according to the penitentials occurred in those populations which had become Christian by mass conversions of peoples along with their rulers and leaders, where the strict catechumenate of the ancient churches was not observed. It leads one to wonder whether penance was perhaps quite frequently sought among such peoples for superstitious motives or from fear of sudden death and terrible punishment after death. Possibly, in the experience of the compilers of those penitentials, penitents seldom came seeking penance with any discernible inclination to lay themselves open to a deep inner conversion and radical transformation by a graciously exigent god. It could be that those compilers seized the opportunity offered by fear and superstition to despatch people on a long journey of repentance in the hope that it would eventually bring them to the point of genuinely seeking penance.

The steps involved in the juncture of the two streams of penance rituals seem actually much smaller than those that had already happened within each stream. Yet the fusion did not take place without tensions and conflicts. The situation of the British churches had been special. From the mid-eighth century we have the testimony of Egbert of York that ever since the days of Theodore of Canterbury it had been the custom of the English church that laymen with their wives and families should visit their confessors each year shortly before Christmas.[4] The aforementioned Theodore, originally from Tarsus, came to England as arch-

[4] O.D. Watkins, *A History of Penance, Vol. II*, p. 644.

bishop of Canterbury in the late seventh century, finding a Celtic Christianity well ensconced to the north and the west more or less peacefully side by side with local churches of Roman origin dating from the Benedictine missions under Augustine of Canterbury. When Theodore arrived and studied the local churches he noted that there was no system of public penance or reconciliation in his new province (meaning probably the whole of England). Theodore noted this without disapproval and lent his name to a penitential that probably contains his own rules though actually written by someone else.[5]

In the *Penitential of Theodore* there is an acknowledgement that both the Greeks and the Romans (that is, in effect, all the ancient churches) have a public reconciliation of penitents on Holy Thursday, but the system of the English is different. There is clearly no intent to make the English system conform. In fact it is spelt out in a way that integrates penance with the existing civil penalties and payments of compensation. Confession to a priest in private seems to be assumed as usual, but there is a note that confession may also be made to God alone (it being understood, it seems, that the same penances will be performed).[6] Reconciliation was apparently also by a priest in private, though no ceremony for it is described. And the custom that Egbert noted had become accepted more or less as an annual obligation for all almost one hundred years later.

On the continent, private penance had already spread through the influence of the Celtic monks and the *Penitential of Columbanus*. This was now followed by the frequent copying and rapid dissemination of the *Penitential of Theodore*. It was given a further boost by St. Boniface and other English missionaries to northern Europe. Finally the custom of repeated private penance, with confession made to priests and reconciliation effected by them, was vigorously promoted by Alcuin of York, English monk-scholar at the

[5]*ibid.*, pp. 647-655.
[6]*ibid.*, p. 653.

court of Charlemagne.[7] The role of the priest in all of these is that of assigning penances and praying that God will forgive the penitent and, apparently, of readmitting the penitent to eucharistic communion.[8]

Also at the court of Charlemagne was Theodulf, a scholar whose training was that of the church of Spain with its far more rigorous idea of maintaining the ancient practice of public penance. Theodulf admits that confession to priests may be helpful for three reasons: that one can obtain counsel, that appropriate penances will be assigned, and that there will be an exchange of prayers. However, he quickly adds that confession to God alone is also good. Moreover, he seems to be arguing against the penitentials in common use, when he exhorts priests to prepare for the ministry of receiving confessions by a pure life and by being properly informed and ready to assign penances in accord with Scripture and the Holy Fathers of the Church. In any case he maintains that for "capital and mortal offences" the ancient discipline of public penance is to be maintained. His position was followed by the Council of Chalon in 813 which also tried to ban the penitentials which by now had multiplied prodigiously.[9] Nevertheless, there is evidence both from the beginning and from the end of the ninth century that the wide diffusion and use of the penitentials, and particularly that of Theodore, continued and that some bishops indeed made it part of their visitations to inquire whether their priests possessed, used and properly understood one of the better known penitentials.[10]

The battle against the penitentials continued unsuccess-

[7]*ibid.*, pp. 688-693.

[8]*Cf.* detailed account according to the *Pseudo-Roman Penitential* in Chapter III and footnote 28.

[9]Watkins, *op. cit.*, pp. 693-698. Its recommendation, however, was not taken up at the conclusive council in Aachen that followed. The Council of Paris in 829 was even more extreme, demanding that all the penitentials be collected and burnt, but it also was unsuccessful in checking the practice of private penance according to the penitentials.

[10]*ibid.*, p. 698 and *cf.* p. 658.

fully. It seems to have been waged basically over the issue of church authority in penance and reconciliation, as exercised by bishops and by ancient church rulings or "canons". The penitentials were frequently attacked on the basis that the errors were certain but their authors unknown. The "certain errors" seem to have been of two sorts — the penitentials contradicted one another and caused confusion, and the penances they listed seemed to be less severe than those of the ancient discipline. The latter accusation is surprising until one realizes the extent to which redemptions and commutations of the penances were commonly allowed. Intended originally to allow quicker completion of penances that would amount to more than a lifetime, or to allow substitutions to people genuinely incapable of performing the penances listed, the system of commutations was clearly liable to abuses. Money payments were accepted in some cases as substitution for personal works of penance (with obvious possibilities for abuse), rich people sometimes hired others to fast for them, and where a literate person might be able to shorten a fast by continuous recitation of the psalms the illiterate were directed to do it by continuously repeated genuflections accompanied by severe flogging.[11]

The chief objection to the penitentials, however, appears to have been their unauthoritative character and the sense that the bishops had very little control over what was going on in private penance administered according to these many varied penitentials. There were even some attempts to produce in their place a compilation of official "canons" governing "the measure" of penance, but the task proved to be impossible and only productive of a few more penitentials no more authoritative than the others.[12]

Meanwhile, however, opposition to the penitentials was not opposition to private penance or confession to priests.

---

[11]For actual examples from primary sources see Paul F. Palmer, *Sources of Christian Tradition, Vol. II, Sacraments and Forgiveness* (Westminster, Md.: Newman, 1959), pp. 145-152, and *cf.* Poschmann, *op. cit.*, pp. 152-153.

[12]Watkins, *op. cit.*, pp. 708-711.

Gradually the principle was established that public penance and reconciliation were appropriate to public sins or crimes but that sins which were not notorious or criminal could appropriately be confessed and repented in private with private reconciliation taking place. Gradually also there seems to have been a change from the pattern in which reconciliation took place at the end of the full performance of the appointed penance. There are some indications that an earlier variant was partial performance of the penance, followed by readmission to eucharistic communion, followed by the performance of the remaining penance. A further variant was a kind of conditional absolution from the penance in case of death intervening before completion. Finally, there began to be the custom of pronouncing the reconciliation at the time of the confession and imposition of the penance even though none of it had yet been performed.[13]

As to the penances imposed, the directives of various councils and synods of the ninth century proved very unhelpful to the priest-confessors. They were at this time repeatedly exhorted to determine the penances by three standards: the Scriptures (which could not have been too helpful), the ancient Canons (which in fact proved to be impossible to compile), and "ecclesiastical custom" (which was precisely what the penitentials had been trying to establish). There was much writing and discussion about making sure that priests knew how to assign penances discriminatingly and appropriately, but in practice there was really no consensus as to what was appropriate or how the priest confessor could determine it concretely. By the tenth century there began to be more general acknowledgement and approval of what had in any case been happening, that is, the assignment of penance at the discretion of the priest confessor who makes his own judgments as best he can.[14] With the acknowledgement of the discretion of the confes-

---

[13]For examples, see Palmer, *op. cit.,* pp. 171-174.

[14]An early directive to this effect is that of the Council of Worms, 868 A.D.

sor and the increasing incidence of reconciliation prior to the performance of the penance, the penances begin to be less and less severe, compared not only to the ancient system of canonical penance but also compared to the tariffs of the penitentials, so that the latter quietly fade out of the picture. At the same time, regular confession becomes widespread and carries no necessary implication of grave sin. It becomes associated particularly with the lenten observance and the preparation for Easter communion, at a time when communion by the laity is infrequent. The regulation of the Fourth Lateran Council of 1215, requiring all Christians who have reached the age of discretion to confess their sins in secret to their own priest at least once a year[15] did not introduce a new custom or a new rite. Nor did the reiteration of it at the Council of Trent in 1551.[16] The rites of the two earlier traditions had merged into a single rite which continued without significant alteration until the post-Vatican II introduction of three different forms of the rite of penance.

Nevertheless, several matters had been determined almost without any discussion or critical reflection — matters that were fraught with consequences. The formula effecting reconciliation had shifted from a prayer to God to forgive (along with a declaration absolving the penitent from further ecclesiastical penalties) to a formula forgiving sin in the name of God by virtue of power vested in the Church by Christ and in the confessor by the Church.[17] In addition to this, the power so vested in the Church was now

[15]For the full text in the original, see Denzinger-Schönmetzer, *Enchiridion Symbolorum* (Freiburg: Herder, 1965), nos. 812-814. For translation of the crucial part of the text, see Palmer, *op. cit.*, pp. 197-198.

[16]For the original text, see *D.S.*, no. 1708 (Canon 8 on Penance). For translation, see Palmer, *op. cit.*, p. 253.

[17]See, for instance, Thomas Aquinas, *Summa Theologiae*, IIIa. q. 84, a. 3. According to Paul Anciaux, there are no indications that the declarative formula was considered obligatory before the thirteenth century. See, *The Sacrament of Penance* (N.Y.: Sheed & Ward, 1962), p. 67. The Decree for the Armenians of 1439, explicitly declaring its obligatory nature, remained the rule. See *D.S.*, no. 1323.

seen as unequivocally linked to priestly ordination. Those who, as in former times, are deeply experienced in the life of the Spirit and have a special charism for reconciliation and conversion of others are now very distinctly barred from the ministry of sacramental or ecclesial reconciliation if they are women or unordained men. Their ministry of guiding others through a conversion, while in itself perhaps deeply and far-reachingly effective, as in the case of Catherine of Siena, for instance, simply "does not count". This is further complicated by the ruling of the Fourth Lateran Council[18] that the required annual confession must be made to "their own priest", that is, the parish priest of the territorial parish. For special reasons permission may be sought from the parish priest to confess to another priest, but unless the former grants his permission there is "no power to bind and loose".

While there were clearly many advantages in combining private and public penance in this way, the three changes just mentioned could obviously make the whole system oppressive and artificial in ways that would not foster true conversion at all. It is certainly helpful for all Christians to acknowledge their sinfulness and continuing need of conversion, but commanding people to do this "on schedule", so to speak, may not be the best way to bring about genuine repentance. Moreover, private confession in the form that has been the official and universal pattern of the sacrament of penance since the Fourth Lateran Council, assumes that guidance in a continuing conversion is being given by the confessor, at least by the choice of penance imposed if no further counsel is given. Therefore, it would seem to be more effective precisely when penitents can seek out notably spiritual and experienced and gifted guides as confessors. The designation of this task as belonging properly to the parish priest in relation to his own parishioners is problematic in several ways. It echoes the situation from the ancient canonical penance. Where the authority of the bishop was previously required to reconcile with the eucha-

---

[18]See footnote 15.

ristic community those whose grave sins had warranted excommunication, the authority of the parish priest is now tightly clamped over each member of the faithful in situations where there is no emergency for the community, no excommunication to lift, no genuine reconciliation with the community to be effected. The possibilities for destructive patterns of domination, that is, of plain bullying, are devastating, especially in smaller and more isolated communities. The well maintained "seal of the confessional", whereby nothing that is learned of the penitent from the confession may be revealed or used outside the confessional under the heaviest penalties[19], is no protection against the bullying that can happen within the confession itself when an insensitive or unscrupulous pastor has his own parishioners as captive annual penitents.

The actual history of the diocesan clergy during and since the Middle Ages lent poignancy and substance to such possibilities. As is well known, in the thirteenth century and later there were recurring rivalries between the diocesan clergy and the mendicant, wandering friars. The latter were generally recognized by the people at large as deeply spiritual men and their ministry of reconciliation and conversion was eagerly sought. Their vocation was to radical poverty and detachment under religious vows, they were more carefully trained in prayer than the diocesan clergy, and frequently they were also more thoroughly grounded in theology and Scripture. With the modern advent of large new apostolic religious congregations of priests, this situation continued and expanded. Moreover the powerful attraction of the monasteries as spiritual centers for the laity survived the cultural changes of the centuries and constantly adapted itself in new forms. In many ways, therefore, the living Spirit in the living Church simply could not be confined within the ironclad system described in the ruling of the Fourth Lateran Council. By the device of "granting faculties" from bishops, relating to the confines of their

---

[19]See footnote 16.

dioceses, whereby priests are authorised to administer the sacrament of penance in the name of the Church, the problem is avoided. Under this system the penitent is not required to ask the parish priest's permission to confess to someone else.

The sheer force of the living Church, that is, of the community of believers, therefore, turned the more legalistic, more public or "canonical" conception of the sacrament of penance, as it was officially from the Fourth Lateran Council to the Second Vatican Council in the western church, to a practical implementation that was more human, more personal, more concerned with conversion. For many it was even concerned with the quest for the perfection of the Christian life by means of regular spiritual direction by a chosen guide. So common was this through the centuries in which individual confession was almost the only known form of the sacrament of penance, that a considerable body of literature pertaining to spiritual direction accumulated.[20]

Yet the legislated pattern of the sacrament shaped the practice of spiritual direction in ways that may not have been entirely helpful. The privacy of confession had led to the custom of constructing confessionals or partitioned cubicles in which priest-confessor and penitent were more or less invisible to each other, allowing for anonymity where the penitent desired it, but imposing a strained and artificial context on the conversation where the penitent was seeking direction and wanted to be recognized. Such confessionals were not universally used but were common enough to constitute a problem. Moreover, the historical merger of the two traditions had left the shape of the rite itself heavily influenced by the notion of court process, judgement and sentence. It was expected that the penitent would enter, probably ask for a blessing, state how long an interval had elapsed since the previous confession, itemize some sins committed in that interval (or, if none came to mind, some

---

[20]An excellent survey and good bibliography is given in Kenneth Leech, *Soul Friend* (London: Sheldon, 1977), Chapter 4, and final bibliography. See also, John T. McNeill, *A History of the Cure of Souls* (N.Y.: Harper & Row, 1951), Chapters VII and XIII.

sins from an earlier time), and speak aloud a memorized or impromptu prayer of contrition for sin. In response to this recital, the confessor was expected to ask questions if something in the confession was not clear, to offer counsel if it seemed appropriate, to impose a suitable penance (which had come to be almost invariably the recitation of some memorized prayers), and to pronounce absolution in the declarative form customary since the thirteenth century.[21]

Because of the theological explanations of the sacrament which had become customary (which will be discussed in the next chapter) the penitent was expected to present in the self-accusation specific and recognizable sins that qualified as "matter for absolution". These confessed sins had somehow to fit into accepted categories. However, the real issues of conversion and the quest for perfection of the Christian life might not fit into these recognizable categories at all. It might not be possible to itemize those issues in a series of discrete acts. The pattern of the rite of individual confession more or less structured the situation so that any spiritual direction that was given would take place within the context of such a confession which was often felt to be artificial and not addressed to the real issues. This reversed the order of the ancient desert and monastic manifestation of conscience from which private confession had been developed. In that original practice it was rather the confession which took place within the context of continuing spiritual direction, and that confession might be of temptations, anxieties, attitudes, situations, rather than specific sinful acts. In this setting the conversation taking place in the process of spiritual direction would also tend to educate and focus the discernment of sinfulness and might pick up specific acts as symptomatic of a more pervasive disorientation.[22]

---

[21]The priest is also required to judge the authenticity of the contrition and purpose of amendment. For the full rite, see *Roman Ritual* of 1614.

[22]For this insight as an interpretation of the past history and the possible future developments, I am particularly indebted to conversational comments of Thomas E. Clarke, S.J. of Woodstock Institute for Theological Reflection at Georgetown University.

A further and perhaps most serious limitation of the rite of the sacrament of penance as it existed in the western church until the Second Vatican Council was that it had become not only private but privatized in the sense of being extremely individualistic in the discernment of sin, in the understanding of the consequences and implications of sin, and in the perception of forgiveness and reconciliation. Indeed the element of reconciliation with the community of the faithful had all but vanished, leaving only the question whether there were institutional excommunications to be lifted, whether there were sins involved that had been "reserved" for reconciliation by the bishop or someone appointed by him, and whether any "mortal" sins were repented with a "firm purpose of amendment" for the future so that there could be readmission of eucharistic communion. But this by-passed the ancient sense of community involvement which made "daily" sins subject to mutual confession and forgiveness both informally and in the recitation of the Lord's prayer. It also by-passed the sense of common involvement in sin which was expressed in the ancient canonical penance by the weeping and prayers of the whole congregation led by the bishop and was expressed in the monastic tradition by the confessor's praying and fasting with the penitent.

It was largely with a view to the above mentioned limitations and distortions that the rite of penance was revised officially after the Second Vatican Council. The Council commissioned a revision of the rite of penance that should more clearly express the nature and effects of the sacrament.[23] This rite was actually drawn up by the Congregation for Divine Worship and officially promulgated by special mandate of the Pope in 1973.[24] It went into effect about two years later when the official translations had been approved

[23] *Sacrosanctum Concilium (The Dogmatic Constitution on the Sacred Liturgy* of Vatican II), no. 72.

[24] For the authorization, theological basis and full text of the rites, see *The Roman Ritual: The Rite of Penance* approved for use in the U.S.A. by N.C.C.B. (N.Y.: Catholic Book Publishing Comp., 1975).

by various episcopal conferences for their particular language and area. The rite has three forms: the rite for the reconciliation of individual penitents, the rite for reconciliation of several penitents with individual confession and absolution, and the rite for reconciliation of several penitents with general confession and absolution.

The rite for the reconciliation of individual penitents is drawn up so as to allow for greeting and informal conversation, followed by a sign of the cross which is intended to mark the beginning of a further conversation more directly and specifically concerned with the penitent's life as a Christian, which is followed in turn by a Scripture reading which leads to the confession. To this confession the priest is able to respond in the context of the conversation that has taken place before, which makes it possible for him to speak to the penitent's life situation as the latter has revealed it and not only to a recital of isolated acts taken out of context. In other words this framework, if followed according to the directions of the ritual, does really make it possible to place the confession in the context of spiritual direction rather than the reverse.

The response that the priest makes to the confession is by way of encouragement and counsel concerning a deeper Christian conversion and concerning specific restitution or redress of injuries to others that may be called for, followed by the imposition of a penance. The penance is supposed to be appropriate to the present stage of conversion needed in the penitent's life, and may consist of prayer or prayers, acts of self-denial, or works of ministering to others (the traditional threefold expression of penitence in prayer, fasting and almsdeeds). The penance is supposed to underscore the social as well as the personal dimension of sin and of forgiveness. The penitent is then expected to signify acceptance of the penance imposed and to express sorrow for sin in response to which the priest pronounces the absolution. The formula of absolution does not go back to the ancient pattern which is purely that of a prayer, but it is broader than the simple declarative form. It begins with a proclamation of the mercy of God in trinitarian terms, prays that through the ministry of the Church God may grant pardon and peace, and absolves in the name of the Trinity. Express provision is made for the choice by the penitent between confession in an open room or behind a screen for anonymity.

In this form of the rite, reconciliation of those in fact cut off from eucharistic communion is provided for and the judgement concerning this is left the responsibility of the confessor. However, the emphasis of the rite is not on this possible need but on the more universal function of the sacrament, namely the fostering of a continuing conversion. The context of Scripture readings and more extensive conversation allows for progressive discovery of and openness to the particular conversion needed. All this is helpful in ways far surpassing the pre-Vatican II rite. However, for the social and ecclesial dimension of both sin and reconciliation-conversion this form of the rite is totally dependent on the personal maturity of understanding of confessor and penitent and on one or both of them deliberately drawing this dimension into the discussion, scripture reading, prayers and imposed penance. The rite itself, in this first form, still has a private and individualistic focus.

This is the reason for the other two forms of the rite. To understand the inner logic of these better it may be well to consider the third before the second. This third rite is the reconciliation of several penitents with general confession and absolution. Such a rite is not new, of course. The *indulgentia* mentioned at the end of Chapter III was precisely a reconciliation of many penitents with general absolution given to the whole congregation in response to a common generic confession of sinfulness and expression of contrition. So was the sermon with absolution delivered by some preachers on major feast days from the eleventh century onwards.[25] So also is the penitential rite at the beginning of the eucharistic celebration even in our day. More

---

[25] *Cf.* Palmer, *op. cit.*, pp. 176-178.

specifically and explicitly such a rite of general confession and absolution was long known and officially tolerated in situations such as that of soldiers going into battle or of people dying in great numbers of epidemics like the plague which was so much feared in medieval Europe.

The third form of the post-Vatican II rite is solidly in the tradition of the above. Its unique character among the three forms of the present rite is that there is no individual confession, and therefore no specific confession of sins, only a generic confession of sinfulness made by the congregation together. As the rite is now drawn up it calls for an introductory song, greeting, explanation of the purpose and significance of the celebration, and prayer. This is followed by three biblical readings and responses as at the Sunday Eucharist, and a homily inviting the congregation to an examination of conscience for which time is allowed. A suitable work of penance is proposed to all. In response to a signal and invitation, the participants express repentance in some way such as kneeling or bowing their heads and recite together a formula which is a general confession of sin and sinfulness such as the *confiteor* followed by the Lord's prayer. The service concludes with a general absolution pronounced over the whole congregation in the same triple form used in the reconciliation of individual penitents, together with a proclamation of praise of God's mercy, a final song and blessing and the dismissal.

This form has much to recommend it. The shape of the rite itself underscores the social and ecclesial dimension of sin and penance. The recitation of the Lord's prayer in connection with the confession of sin has solid warrant in the traditions of the ancient church, as indicated in Chapter II. It brings into focus the ministry of mutual forgiveness of all Christians through which the compassion of the Father expressed in Christ and the Spirit becomes actual and tangible in people's lives. Moreover, the choice of biblical texts, homily topics, suggestions towards examination of conscience and proposal of congregationally suitable work of penance carries a direct challenge to discern the need of conversion in the community — in its life style, priorities and values, interaction among the congregants and relationship with others and with larger social structures. In other words, the quest for suitable matter for the readings and homily should spontaneously draw those who plan the service into reflection on the social and ecclesial dimensions of the particular conversion here needed.

Where such a rite with general absolution is practiced, it does not preclude the individual quest for spiritual direction in the context of a full manifestation of conscience and confession of particular sins, with or without sacramental absolution. Indeed, ideally the first and third rite are used in complementarity. Those who confess regularly may find new dimensions opening up in their understanding of sin and of the issues of conversion in Christ when they take part in an occasional penance celebration, as in Lent and Advent, especially if such a celebration is thoughtfully planned to focus on social and ecclesial aspects. On the other hand, many who have in fact abandoned the practice of confession but whose conscience does not accuse them of serious sin can be challenged not to forget the constant need for discernment of what is sinful and what is redemptive in the world and in one's own life and can be offered practical help in that discernment. This may be all they need. It is certainly often all they will accept. It would seem to be both tragic and unfaithful to the merciful God we know in Jesus Christ not to offer such help to all who stand in need of it.

At present the use of this third rite is hemmed about with many restrictions. These restrictions are concerned mainly with the concept of "mortal sin" and the insistence on "integral confession" at the Council of Trent (which was explicitly not revoked by the Second Vatican Council or by the promulgation of the new forms of the rite of penance[26]). Mortal sin, defined in terms of grave matter, fully understood to be such and deliberately chosen or consented to, constitutes such a rejection of God's love for and claim upon

---

[26] *Cf. Roman Ritual: Rite of Penance* of 1975 for U.S., p. 25.

the sinner that the life of grace, or friendship with God, is not diminished but lost. In this case, the sinner is excluded from eucharistic communion and from the other sacraments until reconciled. The teaching of the Council of Trent is that the sacrament of penance is essential to the reconciliation and that in the sacrament each such "mortal" sin must be explicitly and specifically confessed. The distinction dates from the Middle Ages and became significant in the thirteenth century. It presents considerable problems in our own time because of the realization that sin is not always capsulized in discrete actions but may be in pervasive attitudes, and because we are not at ease with a facile claim to draw neat boundaries between grave and light matter, and because we are even less convinced that clear understanding of sin as sin or deliberate consent to sin as sin is really possible to determine.[27] Nevertheless, the necessity of explicit sacramental confession of all grave sins remains the official teaching, and this has brought about such reluctance to implement the third form of the rite that even those who are quite sure they do not have grave sins on their conscience are not in practice able to avail themselves of this rite.

The present restrictions limit the use of the third form of the rite with general absolution to cases where there is immediate danger of death (such as the traditional ones of the soldiers going into battle and the populations caught in a plague or deadly epidemic) and such other cases as would make it impossible on account of number of penitents and scarcity of priests for people to make individual confessions over long periods of time thereby possibly barring them from eucharistic communion over such long periods of time. Missionary and exceptional situations are envisaged by the rule. The judgement is ordinarily to be that of the bishop. If a priest makes such a judgement in an emergency, he may give general absolution but must promptly report to his bishop that he did so and exactly why. One detects in the

---

[27]See Sean Fagan, *Has Sin Changed?* (Wilmington, Del.: Michael Glazier, 1977), Chapter 4.

way the regulations are set out[28] a certain excess of anxiety lest a custom of giving general absolution in communal penance celebrations should arise by spontaneous demand. The anxiety may be prompted in part by the fact that the inner coherence of the rite is evident, and it commends itself strongly for pastoral reasons. In spite of the above stringent limitations, there is also an instruction that anyone who receives a general absolution under these conditions, having committed grave sin that has not been individually confessed, is still under obligation to confess any such sin individually and explicitly as soon as possible and at least within a year, though such a person may communicate at the eucharist meanwhile.

The second form of the rite of penance is a compromise form needed because of the above restrictions. The order is the same as that of the third form of the rite but after the general confession of sin and recitation of the Lord's prayer by the congregation there is a pause in the community's common celebration during which priests station themselves in nearby confessional rooms or at points in the church out of earshot of others. All who seek absolution then take turns confessing individually, having individual penances imposed and being individually absolved. At the conclusion of the rite, for those who have had time to remain to the conclusion, there is a proclamation of praise of God's mercy, a concluding prayer of thanksgiving and a blessing and dismissal. Obviously, this is manageable though awkward where the congregation is not large and a sufficient number of priest confessors is available. It becomes unmanageable very quickly where the congregations are large and the priests few. In practice, it is reduced to a short penitential prayer service, followed by long confessional lines such as were customary on Saturdays and eves of feasts in large churches under the old system.

Under these circumstances, of course, the members of the congregation treat it as a matter of individual confession

[28]See *Rite of Penance*, 1975, pp. 24-25.

where the priest has no time for personal counsel. Thus, either one comes to the service early, gets in the front of the confessional lines and leaves as soon as absolved, or one comes later, skipping the service so as not to have to wait so long. The communal dimension is quite lost, and this seems to be inherent in the awkwardness of the rite with its general confession and subsequent reiteration in private confession. Nevertheless even this hybrid rite has some advantages over the old system. At least for those who arrive at the beginning there are the scripture readings, the homily and the proposed examination of conscience, so that there is a process of education and challenging of consciences in which social and ecclesial dimensions and pervasive questions of life style and values and priorities can be brought to the attention of people who might otherwise think of sin only in certain very limited conventional categories.

This second, hybrid rite may have other advantages, some of which were probably not foreseen by those who drafted the rite. In at least one large North American city, this rite has brought back into full sacramental communion large numbers of people who had long been totally alienated. The Cardinal had given instructions that such celebrations were to be held in one or more of the large churches during the workers' lunch hour weekly during Lent. In order to accommodate all who came and enable them to return to work in time, priests were instructed to give no counsel, hold no discussion, simply impose penance and absolve. The members of the congregation were instructed to make their confessions as briefly as possible and not to expect any advice. It appears that large numbers of people, who had long been dreading advice and comment and questions about other aspects of their lives on which their own consciences were at peace, rushed to these services for reconciliation as though to a jubilee indulgence.

It is also possible, of course, for those who confess regularly to their own confessors under more leisurely conditions in which guidance is possible, to attend a reconciliation rite according to the second form but without making an individual confession at that time. This is similarly possible for others who, though they do not regularly frequent the sacrament in the individual rite, nevertheless do not feel a present need to make a specific confession of sins or to obtain a sacramental absolution, but who nevertheless want to take advantage of the community reflection on the demands of the Christian life and a community discernment of the needs of continuing conversion. There are many people in this situation. They are usually those whose experiences of priest-confessors have been very unhelpful, perhaps catastrophic, who have found their support and challenge and ministry of reconciliation in the lay community, but who nevertheless yearn for a closer integration into the sacramental life of the Church and wish to live in the context of public community worship.

This need as well as the continuing sense that the communal dimension of sin and conversion needed to be explored led to the practice known for some time under the French title of *revision de vie*, a kind of communal examination of the community's conscience concerning its way of life and values and priorities. This takes place in a context of worship, more especially of scripture readings. In the small groups for which it was devised the actual reflection on sinfulness and conversion could be an informal dialog. In a larger group it proved more workable to make someone responsible beforehand for introducing the reflection with some discernments of his or her own or with a meditation on the biblical reading that would provide a basis for such discernment in the dialog that followed. Such a community worship, which is a kind of penance service without sacramental absolution, requires no clerical leadership and indeed finds its strength precisely in the collegial responsibility and grassroots leadership that emerges.

This custom is taken over by the post-Vatican II ritual as a penitential celebration that is not sacramental in the narrower sense of the term. (No legislation could prevent it from being sacramental in the broader sense of the term as will be explained in the next chapter.) Sample texts for this

are given in the ritual of the U.S. episcopal conference.[29]
They consist of a scripture service with a homily and a proposed examination of conscience, a communal prayer of
repentance and a prayer that God will grant forgiveness of
sins such as is said in the penitential rite at the beginning of
the Eucharist. As here presented, however, they remain a
heavily clerical service in which all real leadership and
initiative is firmly retained in the person of the presiding
priest. Moreover, the instructions repeatedly admonish
priests to warn the congregation that the service is not
sacramental and does not confer absolution. There are
evident inner contradictions in the rites even as we have
them at present, and it is clear that they have not ceased to
evolve in response to the needs of the living Church.

[29]*ibid.,* pp. 178 ff.

Recommended Reading

Kenneth Leech, *Soul Friend: A Study of Spirituality.* (London: Sheldon, 1977), gives a rather full account of the history of spiritual direction and its connection with the sacrament of penance.

Ladislas Orsy, *The Evolving Church and the Sacrament of Penance* (Denville, N.J.: Dimension Press, 1978) discusses the history of change in the sacrament of penance and the possibilities of further change.

Bernhard Poschmann, *Penance and the Anointing of the Sick* (N.Y.: Herder, 1964) is a standard text both for the development of the rites and for the evolving theology which is to be discussed in the next chapter.

Paul Anciaux, *The Sacrament of Penance* (N.Y.: Sheed & Ward, 1962) gives a good brief account of the history of the rites followed by an exposition of the theology of the sacrament as it stood before Vatican II.

Ralph Keifer and Frederick McManus, *The Rite of Penance: Commentaries, Vol. I, Understanding the Document.* (Washington, D.C.: The Liturgical Conference 1975) gives a complete exposition of the new rite.

CHAPTER V

THEOLOGY OF THE SACRAMENT, PAST AND PRESENT

In the strict sense of the term one cannot speak of a theology of the sacrament of penance before the twelfth century. However, there is a significant history from the very beginning of the Christian community, which is a history of explicit and implicit understanding of God's redemptive, healing forgiveness and how it is mediated in the life and prayer of the community. The first observation one makes in looking at this history and trying to understand it is that there is a strong reciprocity of influence between the praxis of forgiving and reconciling and the theoretical understanding of God's forgiveness. Each constantly conditions the other.

The most basic level of praxis could be said to be the death of Jesus, preceding the existence of the Christian community as such. The most basic level of theory might be said to be the understanding of his death which Jesus communicated to his earliest followers by the institution of the Eucharist. The early community certainly understood that Jesus willingly, and after anguished discernment of the Father's will read in the possibilities and limitations of the human situation about him, gave himself up to a brutal, horrifying, contemptuous and utterly unjust death for them. They certainly understood that he did this because he saw it as the way to rescue them from the slavery of sin, and that he was inviting them to do the same for one another. Such is the thrust of the scene of the washing of the feet, the injunctions to follow him by taking up one's cross, his consistent responses to all the situations in which they were quarrelling as to who should be the greater in the Kingdom of Heaven, his program outlined in the Sermon on the Mount and interpreted in the Last Supper discourse, and so forth.

What is not spelt out so clearly and unequivocally is the explanation as to why the death on the Cross is redemptive from sin. The reason for this, of course, is that it is better and more fully understood in the doing of it than in arguments and explanations, and it is better conveyed in stories calling for empathy than in arguments calling for understanding. Hence the New Testament writings and the Gospels in particular are more concerned to show us Jesus in his relationships with the wretched, the broken, the crushed, the sinful, the frightened and inaccessible, those desperately maintaining a facade, the cruel, those bluffing their way through behind hard-set features or painted faces. And because the understanding of what is at stake depends so much on our own participation and on our vulnerability to deeper empathy with the characters in the gospel stories and with the suffering immediately about us in our own life situations, people have in the course of the Christian centuries had a great variety of explanations of what is involved in redemption, in reconciliation or rescue from alienation and unreality, in conversion to God from disorientation.

Yet the Gospels, the Acts of the Apostles and the writings of St. Paul and of John the Evangelist give us some very important indications of the theoretical understanding of the earliest communities. The love of God and the love of the universal "neighbor" are inseparable from each other. The return to God is a community enterprise not accidentally but essentially; return to God is return to authentic community with others. It is the return to vulnerable degrees of empathy and identification with others, transparent or total presence to others, making unreserved common cause with others, sharing of all resources without reserve or qualification, ultimately, therefore, ministry in the deepest sense, that is becoming truly a slave to the needs of others even to the point of all kinds of death to oneself in order to live for others, even to the point of laying down one's life in painful ways.

It is this realization that seems to account for the intensity of the common life of the earliest communities and for the joy and courage which those earliest communities generated in their members. Yet it was clear what their vision and commitment to the Way of Jesus meant in the context of a sinful history in which they themselves were wounded and struggling. It meant not only the once for all grand gesture of renouncing worldly and pagan ways to be baptized into the death of Christ and rise with him to new life in the community. It quite clearly meant the daily struggle against the pull of false values, false needs, exclusivity and self-promotion at the expense of others. It clearly meant coping with daily failure and therefore it meant meeting the daily challenge to mutual forgiveness. It is surely this awareness that gave such a central place to the recitation of the Lord's prayer as the daily, efficacious sign of forgiveness and reconciliation with God in the patristic church. Likewise, it is this awareness that the task of forgiveness is the most basic task of the Church which makes the Eucharist the summit of Christian life, the efficacious sign of the fruitfulness of the death of Jesus in the continuing conversion of the members of his bodily presence in the world. It is a conversion in which in a true sense they no longer live but Christ lives in them in as much as they are dying to themselves but alive to him, to others, to the community in a continuing experiment of mutual reconciliation mediating the reconciliation with God.

It is in this context, though gradually losing the universal fervor of the earliest communities, that the Christians had to solve the question as to what to do about the gravely scandalous, and solved it in fact by deciding that reconciliation must be possible because Jesus died for us all while yet we

were sinners and "enemies" of God. It is in this context that
they mapped out the return in terms of gradual reintegra-
tion into the eucharistic community as described in earlier
chapters. It is in this context also that a distinction was
made in the theory of repentance and conversion between
the harsh human rule of the once only return into the
community and the seventy times seven boundlessness of
the ultimate forgiveness of God to whose mercy even those
were earnestly recommended by the Church for whom no
further ecclesial reconciliation was deemed possible. For
even they were bidden to fast and pray and give themselves
to works of charity and mercy with confidence in the ever-
lasting mercy of God, and eventually the Church expressed
this concretely by allowing repeated reconciliation on the
deathbed.[1] Moreover, it is in this context that the invidious
distinction between a class of official sinners and a class of
the officially faithful in the Church gradually disappeared
again and the various rites previously described expressed
the conviction of universal sinfulness even after baptism and
universal need of continuing conversion and reconciliation.

One important aspect of the patristic theology of repentance and forgiveness as mediated by the Church is the
question of the "power of the keys" or the question of
"loosing and binding". This thorny question has plagued the
theology of penance and reconciliation down to the present
time and was a crucial factor in the issue of "integral"
confession that became so large and troublesome a matter at
and after the Council of Trent. The phrase "power of the
keys" and the notion of "loosing and binding" have reference, of course, to Mt. 16:13-20. In this gospel text "binding
and loosing" are technical rabbinical terms having reference
to a "bond" of excommunication and the "dissolving" of the
bond of excommunication. There is no doubt whatever that

---

[1]For the details of this history see excerpts from primary sources in Paul F.
Palmer, *Sources of Christian Tradition, Vol. II. Sacraments and Forgiveness.*
(Westminster, Md.: Newman, 1959) *e.g.* p. 88, p. 125. And *cf.* O.D. Watkins, *A
History of Penance, Vol. I.* pp. 475 ff., and Bernhard Poschmann, *Penance and the
Anointing of the Sick* (N.Y.: Herder, 1964), sections III and IV.

this is the sense in which the patristic church was applying the idea in the ancient public or canonical penance. A public sinner was bound by the bond of excommunication and by the terms or conditions to be fulfilled before that bond would be dissolved. The question that arose, even in the writings of the Church Fathers, concerned the connection between this judicial action of the institutional representatives of the Church and the judgment of God.

This question arose in relation to some positions taken by Tertullian after he became a Montanist and entered into contention with the Catholic Church from a more rigorist position.[2] It also came up in the writings of Hippolytus[3], Cyprian[4], Clement, and Origen of Alexandria[5], and again in the West with Pope Leo I[6] and with Augustine[7]. What emerges rather consistently in spite of other sharp differences in the positions of these authors is that the power of loosing and binding belongs to the Church as a whole, that is the whole living community of the faithful, though exercised by bishops and sometimes by priests on their behalf.[8] Secondly, there is a constant assumption of an organic connection between membership in the Church and entrance into the Kingdom, though it is neither analyzed nor spelt out. The connection is evidently not the simplistic one which would have the institutional church authorized to make judgments in this life and world which will then be carried out by God after death in another life and world simply because God decreed this and bound himself to carry out the judgments of human judges in his ultimate dealings with other human persons. There is a very strong sense in

[2]Poschmann, *op. cit.*, pp. 48-49.

[3]*ibid.*, p. 52.

[4]*ibid.*, pp. 58-62.

[5]*ibid.*, pp. 64-75.

[6]*ibid.*, pp. 99-100.

[7]*ibid.*, pp. 101-102.

[8]This is the judgement of Poschmann and seems well founded, *cf. op. cit.*, pp. 101-102.

the patristic writings of the absolute majesty and otherness of God, and an acceptance of mystery and of human limitation. Moreover there is a continuous awareness that the mercy of God exceeds our imaginings.

Yet there is evident conviction that there is a connection between the binding and loosing of the Church and the implementing of the mercy of God. In general, the Fathers of the Church are satisfied to propose the relationship in paradoxical terms and to leave it there. We can probably do no better than follow their example. Yet it may not be remiss to point out that if the whole Church and all its life and worship and exchange and mutual support are seen as sacramental, that is, as efficacious sign of grace and salvation, there is an evident present connection between access to the Kingdom or Reign of God and effective practical sharing in the life and worship of the Church. There is nothing esoteric or strange about this connection. The Church is the bodily presence of the risen Jesus continuing the work of rescuing us from the slavery of sin and despair and confusion. The Church is the communion and community of the followers of Jesus with him and with one another in the power of the Spirit. This is realized very concretely in all dimensions of everyday life, in which our lives become open to transformation in the Spirit. To be drawn into the practical exchange and support of this community is to have the gates of heaven opened to one. To be excluded is to have the ordinary and easy access to the coming Reign of God closed in one's face. Only the gravest considerations of scandal to the community or challenge to the conscience and self-knowledge of the transgressor could justify such an action, but the possibility and consequences of the action are clear.

Another issue that arises for us as we look at the evidence from the patristic era and which became an important issue in the mediaeval understanding of penance is the question as to what it is that constitutes the efficacious sign of forgiveness and reconciliation. The patristic church appears to place equal emphasis on the personal conversion of the sinner and the reconciling response of the Church. This is so both in the practice and theory of public penance (which should be evident from the preceding chapters) and in what is written and done concerning the "daily" sins and the forgiveness extended mutually and sought in the constant recitation of the Lord's prayer and in the eucharistic celebration.[9] Reconciliation has, of course, two distinct though related meanings which have continued into the present time and account for the post-Vatican II emergence of the preferred term, "sacrament of reconciliation". Reconciliation can have a technical, juridical sense of readmission to full communion of the formerly officially excommunicated. It can, however, have the much broader and more profoundly human meaning in our relations with one another as with God that there has been a shadow, a tension, a contradiction in the relationship and that this awkwardness or breach in the relationship is now healed. In this broader sense reconciliation is the other side of the coin of conversion and repentance, no matter what the nature and effect of the sin in the community.

That the conversion was seen as equally important is clear from the rigor of the penances thought appropriate both in the patristic and in the mediaeval period. While there is constant explicit reference to the inner conversion of heart, symbolized by the oft-mentioned "weeping and lamenting", there is evident conviction that such inner conversion of heart is not attained in a vacuum but in solid and arduous works of penance, under the generic categories of prayer, fasting and almsdeeds, which should effect a deep and pervasive change in the future character of one's everyday life and conduct in the world. That the grace of God is not so much a reward for this effort as the original condition of its possibility in the first place seems to be taken for granted in most of the Church Fathers and expressed in the practice of

[9]*Cf.*Godfrey Diekmann, "Reconciliation through Prayer of the Community", in Nathan Mitchell, ed. *The Rite of Penance: Commentaries, Vol. III.* (Washington, D.C.: Liturgical Conference, 1973).

passionate prayer of the bishop and the community on behalf of the penitents. In the writings of Augustine of Hippo it becomes a pervasive explicit theme.

The more formal theology of the sacrament of penance may be said to have begun in the twelfth century, which provided a framework for sacramental theology generally and established the enumeration of the sacraments as seven among which was reckoned penance. In this context it became necessary to set out what were the "essential parts" of the sacrament and what was their relation to one another. It was now customary to effect the reconciliation, that is pronounce the absolution, at the time of the confession. This raised the objection that forgiveness and reconciliation could not be the outcome of the "satisfaction" or works of penance, because they had not been performed yet. So the focus shifted from satisfaction to contrition, or authentic sorrow for sin. This was not altogether an innovation, of course, because the patristic and earlier mediaeval testimonies had seen the inner conversion of the heart as the essential reality which was expressed or realized in the works of penance. Yet there remained now the obvious problem that it is one thing to say, "I am sorry", and mean it, but a far more laborious and demanding matter really to put right what one regrets, really to make sorrow for sin actual and operative in one's life.

The next step was obvious enough, though the cause of much trouble and confusion over the centuries. A distinction had to be made now, which was not necessary under the older systems of canonical penance or tariff penance. It was the distinction between the essential forgiveness of the sin, or the guilt of the sin, on the one hand and the remission of "punishment" or penance required on the other. It seems, as one reads the arguments and debates that took place that the works of penance take on more and more the aspect of a certain measure of punishment that is due, a certain allotment of retributive suffering to be inflicted and undergone, a certain vengeance to endure to make the scales of justice balance. This led to some complicated and some very bitter arguments, which will not here be presented in detail.[10] What is here selected is only what appears to be helpful towards an understanding of the issues we face in the present practice and theory of the sacrament of penance.

Some of the arguments that took place were due to the changing formula of absolution, because like previous teachers and writers the scholastic authors theologized from the data of their own experience of the Church and its life and worship. Formerly absolution had commonly been a prayer that God would forgive, accompanied by a declarative absolution from further penances and penalties. Now the declarative formula is coming more sharply into focus and it begins to appear as though the priest confessor claims not to absolve from penalties or penances but simply from the sins. Thus though Peter Abelard and Peter the Lombard both seem to place the focus on the penitent's contrition to which God responds by granting forgiveness, the Victorines, Hugh and Richard, put the priest in the center of the focus, forgiving sins in the proper sense of that term because God had given the power of the keys to priests as successors of the apostles. It may be conjectured that when the Victorines quoted Mt. 16:19 they were not aware of the rabbinic sense of binding and loosing and assumed the terms simply meant forgiving sin in the name of God.[11]

The Lombard deals with the question of the power of the keys by inferring (also without knowing the rabbinic sense) that there must be one sense in which God forgives and another in which the priest forgives. He cannot accept a view of God in which God would refuse forgiveness and remission of "eternal punishment" to anyone who repented. Therefore he infers that the priest's binding and loosing has

---

[10]The detailed history can be found in Poschmann, *op. cit.*, Ch. Three, sections IX-XI. A far more readable account which is thorough and accurate but unfortunately not footnoted is given by Joseph Martos, *Doors to the Sacred* (N.Y.: Doubleday, 1981), Ch. IX, section 3. A good selection of primary sources is available in Palmer op. cit., section 4.

[11]The details are set out by Martos, *op. cit.*, and *cf.* Palmer, *op. cit.*, pp. 186-192.

to do with excommunications and imposition of penance.[12] The Lombard also takes the opportunity to ask whether it is useful to confess to a lay person and concludes that it is useful, more especially when it is not possible to confess to a priest.[13] Yet it is more useful to confess to a priest because he has the key of knowledge and the key of power, to judge and to impose the proper penance and therefore to certify that God has forgiven, a model that he takes over from Anselm of Canterbury.[14]

In the debates that continued at this time there was in effect a preoccupation with the question, "What difference does the sacrament make?" Granted that contrition and God's forgiveness are the opposite sides of the same coin, a point on which many of these authors up to and including Albert the Great are firmly agreed, then what is the efficacy of the sacrament for forgiveness? Even Thomas Aquinas experienced considerable difficulty with that question for the same reason that the Lombard did and that we do today. How tenuously the forgiveness of God is connected to the absolution and the power of the keys for Thomas is under-scored by the fact that he allows a lay person to administer the sacrament in case of necessity and considers it an obliga-tion in some circumstances to confess to a lay person.[15] Yet Thomas is concerned to justify the efficacy of the sacrament for forgiveness because his experience of the Church's cele-bration of the sacrament convinces him that that is what is being claimed in the action itself and in the Church's teach-ing of its necessity. In spite of a very awkward deferral to the Master of the Sentences, that is Peter the Lombard, Thomas seems to resolve the issue by seeing the sacrament as the means of disposing the penitent in true contrition for the remission of sins, giving the sacrament a kind of power to attract sinners to repentance by the outreach of grace in the

---

[12]For relevant excerpts from primary source, see Palmer, *op. cit.,* pp. 194-196.
[13]*ibid.,* p. 194.
[14]*Cf.* Poschmann, *op. cit.,* p. 160 ff.
[15]*Summa Theologiae.* Supplement, q.8, a.2 & 3.

sacrament.[16]

In this mediaeval understanding of the sacrament of penance there had come to be three levels, so to speak. At the outer layer, or superficial level, there was the evident activity of the penitent's confession and expression of contrition and of the confessor's imposition of penance and absolution. This level was sometimes referred to as the mere sign. At a deeper level was the penitent's genuine contrition, which would include the purpose of amendment of life by turning away from the sin in practice. That was referred to as the reality to which the outer sign pointed, but which was in turn a sign of a still deeper reality. It would also be possible to place at this level the specific grace of the sacrament disposing the penitent to contrition. At the deepest level or inner core of the sacrament was that which was the ultimate reality and did not point any further, namely God's forgiveness. This seems to be a very helpful scheme: the external activity of the sacrament is there for the purpose of disposing the penitent to true contrition, and the inner experience of contrition has as its purpose to open the penitent to the reconciling and healing grace of God.

The official Catholic doctrine of the sacrament of penance subsequently received its definitive shape from the Council of Trent, a teaching which was not substantially altered by the Second Vatican Council or by the decree promulgating the new forms of the rite. The official teaching to this time is as follows. There is a separate sacrament of penance for the forgiveness of sins committed after baptism. It is truly a sacrament, that is a sign that is efficacious in conferring the grace it signifies (namely forgiveness of sin) because it is the action of Christ himself in the Church and owes its origin to him as attested by Scripture. This sacrament is necessary for the forgiveness of grave sins (which

---

[16]*ibid.,* q.18.a.1. The total teaching of Thomas on the sacrament of penance is extremely complex and appears to have changed from his earlier to his more mature writing. An attempt to trace it in detail is made by Poschmann, *op. cit.,* pp. 168-183, compared with the Scotist doctrine on pp. 184-193.

must be individually and specifically confessed) even though such forgiveness may take place before the actual celebration of the sacrament if an act of perfect contrition is made with the intention of confessing later when it becomes possible. The constituent parts of the sacrament are: on the part of the penitent, contrition, confession and satisfaction (together considered as the "quasi-matter" of the sacrament), and on the part of the minister of the sacrament the absolution formula, "I absolve you, etc." (considered as the "form" of the sacrament, in the Aristotelian sense of the term or an adaptation of it). The proper minister of the sacrament is an ordained priest who has been granted the faculty of jurisdiction for the class of persons he claims to absolve by the competent bishop. In emergencies, such as danger of death, a priest may absolve without such a specific grant of jurisdiction.[17]

Some contemporary theologians and Catholic intellectuals have had some difficulty with several points in this teaching. One of these is the claim that the sacrament of penance was "instituted" by Christ himself. When this was disputed by some scholars at the beginning of the present century, the objection was condemned by Pope Pius X in 1907 as part of the errors of Modernism.[18] It seems unnecessary to quarrel over this point. It is clear that in the broad sense the sacrament of penance owes its origin to Jesus himself in his ministry of reconciliation and forgiveness which he entrusted to the Church. It also seems clear from the history as set out in earlier chapters of this book that the ministry of reconciliation and forgiveness developed from that original source in the ways that were apt according to the times and that there is a certain coherence in the growth and development which the believer may with justification attribute to the Spirit of Jesus alive and active in the living Church which is his bodily presence. In the light of Resur-

---

[17]For the original text of Session XIV of the Council of Trent, on Penance and Anointing, see *D.S.* 1667-1719. For translation of more significant sections, see Palmer, *op. cit.,* pp. 239-254.

[18]*D.S.* 3446-3447.

rection faith, quibbles over the exact formulation of the origin of the sacrament seem petty and inappropriate. There seems to be no reason to deny either what we know of the history of the developments in the rite or the doctrinal claim of its origin in the personal mandate of Jesus.[19]

Closely connected with the objection is the problem some have had with the claim that the form of the sacrament is in the words "I absolve you, etc.". The objection is made that that formula did not exist from the beginning and that when it did arise it had reference not to absolution from sin in the sense of forgiveness, but to absolution from further penances and penalties. Again it would seem to be possible to acknowledge this history but note that the Fathers of the Council of Trent were defending the faith and practice of the Church as they knew it, that is, as it was in their time and that they were defending the only form of the sacrament of penance with which they were familiar.[20] As a matter of fact, neither Vatican II nor its post-conciliar commissions and decrees of promulgation saw fit to change the words of the central formula. That may have been because they thought of them as permanently binding. There seems to be no good reason for insisting on this.[21] It could be changed in future adaptations of the rite.

The final and most painfully urgent issue that has been raised concerning the continuing teaching of the Tridentine position has to do with the requirement of "integral confession", that is the condition that specific confession of any mortal sins coming to mind after careful examination of conscience is required for absolution to be effective and also for divine forgiveness. The issue is more substantive than the other two because it places such a concrete demand on

[19] *Cf.* Carl Peter, "Integral Confession and the Council of Trent", in E. Schillebeeckx ed., *Concilium, Vol. 61. Sacramental Reconciliation* (N.Y.: Herder, 1971).

[20] *Ibid., passim.*

[21] *ibid.,* and *cf.* also James McCue, "Penance as a Sacramental Sign", and Frans Heggen, "The Service of Penance", both in the same volume. For contrary opinion, see Z. Alszeghy, "Problemi dogmatici della celebrazione communitaria", *Gregorianum,* 48 (1967).

"the faithful" and claims to put them in bad faith if they do not meet it. The objections to this teaching are: that there is no historical justification for claiming such obligation as being of divine institution, rather than simply a disciplinary rule of the Church; that there is no pastoral justification, because true repentance can in fact take place without priestly or sacramental intervention, as it does among Christians of other denominational communities, sometimes with spectacularly evident effect; that it rests upon a definition of mortal sin that is rapidly becoming less and less tenable; and finally, that it may be impossible to know all one's serious sins, if these are not thought of as plainly discernible discrete acts but in terms of fundamental option or in terms of underlying and pervasive attitudes such as racism, systematic oppression of the poor and powerless, a radically and systematically unmerciful attitude, a livelihood and life-style based on warmongering or on the promotion of pornography or destructive drugs or other dehumanizing artifacts.

These are real objections and they should be dealt with one by one, as they will be in another context in the following chapters. However, the decrees of the Council of Trent appear to be the wrong context in which to consider them, for the reason already stated above. The Fathers of Trent obviously intended to defend the practice and doctrine of the Church's sacraments as they knew them in their time. They wanted to justify their place in the continuity of Christian tradition and, out of their own experience and understanding and piety, they explained how they saw these practices and teachings to be rooted in the Scriptures. Living in circumstances they could not have foreseen, with more detailed historical knowledge of earlier forms of the rite, and with practical experience of the new forms now in use, our generation or the next may well adapt the teaching in ways more apt to foster genuine conversion and deeper Christian community in the changing life of the Church.[22]

---

[22]This is, as I understand it, substantially the position of Carl Peter, *op. cit.,* which seems to me the more reasonable interpretation of the authority of the Tridentine teaching for our times and the future.

Meanwhile, legislators and pastors of the Church would certainly be well-advised to take note of the fact that increasing numbers of very dedicated Christians, occasionally heroic Christians, are finding it compatible with their consciences to absent themselves permanently or for long periods of time from the sacrament of penance while regularly communicating at the Eucharist and simultaneously practicing contraception or living in full marital relationship in a second marriage during the life time of the first marriage partner, or in some other way making choices of conscience which the official teaching would designate as mortally sinful. Likewise it is not uncommon that even those who have repented of living in concubinage or of sexual promiscuity or of deep involvement in drugs, acknowledging that their past life was seriously sinful, joyfully celebrate a private conversion and readmit themselves to eucharistic communion without further ado. There is an overwhelming sense among the more educated Catholics that "what counts" is the living reality of one's relationship with God and that where rituals help they are to be used and where they hinder they are to be ignored.

Under these circumstances, it is hardly adequate to pronounce condemnations, because the condemnation can only arise out of that very perception of the mediation of God's grace and healing forgiveness in the world which has been so deliberately abandoned by these people with a sense of liberation and new faith and hope and surrender to God's call as they have heard it. One must rather find ways in which the sacramental rites can be experienced as authentically mediating the grace of conversion and reconciliation. The remaining chapters of this book will be devoted entirely to several dimensions of this.

Recommended Reading

See bibliographies for Chapters III and IV and the following:

Joseph Martos, *Doors to the Sacred* (N.Y.: Doubleday, 1981). This is very informative and easy to read. It gives an especially clear account of the theological history.

Nathan Mitchell, ed. *Rite of Penance: Commentaries, Vol. III* (Washington, D.C.: Liturgical Conference, 1973). This contains important essays on history and interpretation.

Edward Schillebeeckx, ed. *Concilium, Vol. 61. Sacramental Reconciliation* (N.Y.: Herder, 1971). This is particularly helpful on the possibilities of further development.

CHAPTER VI

THE EFFICACY OF THE SACRAMENT: RECONCILIATION AND CONVERSION

It is clear that the task of adapting the rite of the sacrament of penance to the needs of our times is not finished. Moreover, as with the adaptation in the rite of the Eucharist and that of baptism, it is becoming clear that there is much more at stake than tinkering with the formula, no matter how expertly and wisely. The rallying cry of the liturgical movement before, during and after the Second Vatican Council was the slogan, "the signs should signify". This does go to the heart of the issue but only because the slogan means far more than is at first sight evident.

That the signs should signify does, of course, mean that language should not be obscure or misleading, that stories and images should be such as can be understood, that the actions of the ritual should really express in the experience of the people participating what they are supposed to express. But all of this is by no means sufficient. Nor is it really at the heart of the matter. The signifying of the signs goes much deeper than this into the whole life of the Church, the relationships among its members, the goals toward which its efforts are turned, the experience it mediates of the welcome of God, the compassion of Christ, the power of the Spirit. This is the level at which the signification is authentic or inauthentic, and it is a level which cannot be ignored in the attempt to revitalize the sign of the sacrament of penance. Interestingly enough, it is also the level of reality at which institutional structures, rules, restrictions are least operative either to help or to hinder. This level is really wide open to the creativity of the community.

Those who are alienated from sacramental reconciliation in our times are in many different situations and in many frames of mind. They include those who stay away from all community worship, those who stay away completely from the sacrament of penance but only from that, those who stay away from the sacrament of penance and therefore feel themselves obliged to refrain from eucharistic communion also, those who come perhaps once a year out of some residual unwillingness to drop the practice while nevertheless unable to make any sense of it, and those who frequent the sacrament with a certain sense of desperation because they know it ought to make sense and yet their experience is that it does not. Extensive interviews with many such people who were willing to talk about it yielded one common trouble: these people, including those who come anyway, after careful observation, have concluded that sacramental penance does not make any difference. Their experience is that it is a sign of something that it does not effect. In other words, it is not an efficacious sign, and therefore not a sacrament according to the standard definition.

Under an older way of thinking about sin, grace and salvation, there would be an easy answer to this. The effect is hidden. It is supernatural. It is not subject to direct observation. Yet we know that something really happens, because the Church teaches us so and the Church, which received its teaching from Christ through the Apostles, is also guided from error by the Holy Spirit and therefore teaches only the truth. There is a sense in which all of this is correct, but it is not that facile sense which could eliminate the question concerning the change that is not experienced in connection with the sacrament of penance. In the context of contemporary theology of grace[1] and sacramental theology[2] and in the context of a more contemporary understanding of sin[3] and of the ways sin is manifested or experienced, it is no longer simply true to say that the effects of the sacraments are by nature outside the range of direct experience. The working of grace in our lives has to be understood in a more nuanced way. This understanding has already become widely diffused and has been joyfully received because it responds so fully to contemporary experience of human existence in its many dimensions. Therefore, many people who have never read any sacramental theology and may have had little catechetical instruction in the sacraments nevertheless have a very shrewd and clear intuitive sense of the difference which the sacraments ought to be making in their lives if they really are sacramental. By the same token they are cannily disinterested in a sacramental celebration which makes them as vulnerable as the sacrament of penance does, if it is not in fact efficacious in ways that respond to a very deep human need.

The deep human need to which the sacrament is addressed is the need to return to the Father's house from exile, to come home to one's true place, to find liberation from fear, boredom and frustration, to find one's authentic existence behind the many masks of unreality, to find peace from restlessness, anxiety and discontent, to find a bottomless inner peace with God, with other people and all fellow creatures, with one's own dependency and limitations and with the uncertainty of the future and the certainty of death.

[1]The key authors are: Henri de Lubac and Karl Rahner. The thought of both can be found in a variety of essays published in different collections, as well as in longer works. A good summary of the shift in understanding is given by Charles R. Meyer, "Grace", in George J. Dyer, ed., *An American Catholic Catechism* (N.Y.: Seabury, 1975).

[2]Probably the best exposition is that of Edward Schillebeeckx, *Christ, the Sacrament of the Encounter with God.* (N.Y.: Sheed & Ward, 1963).

[3]A far reaching re-examination of the notion of sin is Piet Schoonenberg, *Man and Sin* (Notre Dame, Ind.: University of Notre Dame Press, 1965). A very coherent and readable contemporary presentation is Sean Fagan, *Has Sin Changed?* (Wilmington, Del.: Michael Glazier, Inc., 1977).

Of this need all are in greater or lesser degree aware. Sin manifests itself in suffering. Sin as sin is not directly accessible to experience, though Bible and tradition teach us to identify it as the disorientation that leaves our lives turned away from God and therefore lacking in focus and integration. What is directly accessible to experience is the restlessness, the discontent, the fear and diffuse anxiety, the inability to live in harmony and community with others, the inability to accept our own dependency, poverty and limitations. And these things come into direct observation in particular encounters, particular happenings, particular failures and tragedies.

Many people today experience a keen need and desire to be "led home" to an authentic existence, a deep inner conversion of their whole being to the ultimate truth that is God, an all-embracing personal surrender to the creating, regenerating and welcoming love of God. But for the most part they are wandering about like sheep without a shepherd from psychiatrist to T-group, from yoga to tai chi, from mantra chanting to transcendental meditation, from pornography to poetry, from alcohol to drugs, from communes and open marriages to divorce, from fierce competition to "dropping out", from restlessness to despair. Even with the materially comfortable, the apparently stable, the suave, the elegant, the suburban middle class, the frightened awareness that all is not well lies very close to the surface under a shallow guise of respectable normalcy. Except that we of the western and more industrialized countries today enjoy a higher material standard of living, these people seem not to be very different from the crowds to whom Jesus preached the immediate nearness of the Reign of God and the conversion by which one might enter the Kingdom.

As such people have experienced the sacrament of penance, it does not seem to offer them hope of reconciliation in the deep human and spiritual sense in which they are aware of their need. Beginning with an examination of conscience in order to come up with a list of recognizable transgressions simply seems irrelevant. Those who manage it, recite the list, are given prayers to say and are pronounced "absolved", frequently know with a bitter sense of emptiness and discouragement that the whole event has not touched the reality of their lives and therefore has no power to bring the reconciliation they seek. They do not think of forgiveness of sins in juridical categories. The fear of hell is no longer a reality for many Catholics. The hope of heaven has become something more subtle, more shrouded in the mysteries of death and of God's transcendence. Many people have abandoned any sense of secret accounts being kept of their good and bad behavior with a view to reward and punishment later. They are concerned with reconciliation in a more human, more personal and therefore more spiritual sense.

It does not seem too fanciful to suggest that what such people are searching for corresponds rather closely to the three levels of sacrament of which the mediaeval theologians spoke and wrote: the level of the mere sign (which exists only to point to the reality); the level that is already part of the reality (though it points further); and the level that is pure reality (and therefore has to be manifested in sign so that we may know it is there). When people come to confession, recite a list of transgressions and are given absolution, they frequently have the sense that the middle level is missing. The outer signs are expected to signify and mediate reconciliation with the unseen God without any inner experience of integration, focus, liberation, conversion (which would already be part of the reality that is signified and would therefore powerfully point further to the reality that cannot be experienced directly). It seems as though the ritual itself is supposed to be sign and pledge enough, without any personal transformation. But people are not satisfied with this hollow sign.

Of course, one could simply respond that this shows a lack of faith in sacramental grace which is, after all given by virtue of the action that is done which is the action of Christ himself (*ex opere operato,* as we used to say, thinking that by dint of keeping it in Latin we could bypass the obvious questions). But this teaching, which goes back to Augustine

of Hippo, has to do with the problem of unworthy cele-
brants presiding over sacramental celebrations. It is not
concerned with whether there can be grace in a person's life
without personal transformation. Grace *is* personal transformation. Therefore a person can not be graced without
being transformed. In other words a person can not be
graced without the effects of it becoming accessible to experience.[4] There seems to be an urgent truth, therefore, in the
sense of deprivation with which people respond to the hollow sacraments in which the middle level of experienced
personal transformation seems to be missing. They are not
thinking of salvation as future reality and grace as hidden
bookkeeping. They are understanding salvation in a far
more biblical sense as total personal, even communal,
rescue from disorientation, alienation, frustration. Therefore, they understand grace as the merciful intervention of
God by which that rescue is genuinely, presently, gradually
being effected. They understand it very literally and fully as
saving grace, and they expect to experience it.

It would seem to be a matter of the gravest urgency to ask
why so many people do not experience the power of God's
healing in the sacrament of penance, and even more urgent
to consider how the lack might be made good. It may be
helpful to look at the situations, celebrations, relationships
and events in which people *are* finding the healing power of
God mediated in their lives. Probably the most common of
these is a group of seekers in which there is a peer group
relationship, that is a group that is not assembled around an
authority figure. Such are prayer groups, Bible study
groups, groups explicitly built around the *revision de vie,*
sometimes even action-reflection groups which begin with a
task outside the group and gradually find that they have to
reflect on where they themselves stand individually and in
their relations with one another in the group.

What frequently happens in such groups is that by common prayer, meditation, friendship and action, a level of

[4]See footnote 1.

trust and common faith is built up in the context of which people are able to confide their unanswered questions, their anxieties, their frustrations and resentments and sufferings to one another. In a good atmosphere this leads to confessions of personal failure and sinfulness, sometimes of specific sins, either to the group or to some helpful member of the group. Under such circumstances there is often a real conversion and genuine human reconciliation mediated by the prayer and support of the group members. Such conversions are readily expressed in appropriate works of repentance because their foundations are deep and solid and they have continuing support from the group. Groups such as Alcoholics Anonymous, whether explicitly religious or not, are built on this principle and effect profound and lasting conversions and reconciliations in the lives of their members.

Such groups often have another dimension. Not only do they reach into the individual lives of the members in a healing and reconciling way by prayer, friendship and practical works of mercy, but they often awaken deeper levels of conscience in the community as such concerning its life-style and issues of social justice and public responsibility. People who pray deeply and experience their rootedness in God together seem gradually to be infused with the courage to take a more discerning, more Christian look at the social and public dimensions of their lives, and with the freedom to act healingly and compassionately in the public order. We have long had before us the example of Quaker and certain Anabaptist groups undertaking very radical and heroic tasks in society in a spirit of cheerful serenity born of this kind of rootedness in community prayer. In many places the JOCiste movement had just such an impetus among Catholics, and sometimes the Sodalities did. There are many such groups springing up locally and quite spontaneously and they are, in the broad sense of the term, true and effective sacraments of reconciliation and conversion.

Probably equally common, though there is no way to know this of course, is that kind of lay and often mutual confession that takes place over the kitchen table between neighbors and friends used to giving one another support and encouragement. Attention has often been drawn to the possibility of destructive gossip in such circumstances, but there are probably far more healing encounters than harmful ones of this type. Many women who are quiet centers and anchors in their own homes have special gifts of healing, discernment, calling to repentance and reconciliation. In an unofficial and utterly unpretentious way there are many little domestic churches where a basic and authentic ministry of reconciliation and conversion is going on.

The dynamic of it seems to be very simple, very close to the experience of the desert fathers. There is a person who is deeply prayerful, rooted in the loving presence of God, at peace with herself in her dependence and limitations and essential poverty, and at peace with the rest of creation. She is there, she has time, the coffee pot is usually on and her whole being speaks welcome. And people come, as they did to the elders in the desert, with their troubles, their anger, their hurt and their shame. She hears them out with compassion, she counsels them from her experience and her prayer, sometimes she effects by her unpretentious mediation of grace a conversion of heart that mends a marriage, saves a family, changes a life. Always she lets them know by her own response that God loves them and that they are welcome back. Always she accompanies them with her prayers when they have left. She would be startled if told that she is ministering a sacrament of reconciliation and conversion, but in the broad sense of the word that is what she does, and the Church is built and maintained by ministries such as these.

Another experience that is frequently an efficacious sign of reconciliation and conversion for people today is a retreat — perhaps a week-end in a country setting in an atmosphere of silence and continuous prayer, or perhaps a group assembled for a few days to share their meditations on a particular theme in depth, perhaps even a preached retreat consisting of sitting in a chapel listening to conferences, or, for the privileged few, a directed retreat in which their personal meditations are guided into pathways of deepening prayer and more effective surrender to the will of God in their everyday lives. Many people find that when they make a confession in the context of a retreat it takes on the palpable character of a conversion. Even if they do not make a confession in the course of the retreat, they are often vividly conscious that the retreat has mediated a conversion for them. That this is authentic and not fanciful is evidenced by the fact that people so often implement the inner conversion of a retreat in very solid changes in their lives, through works of repentance in the classic categories of prayer, self-denial and charity, and through the way they handle the daily circumstances and demands of their lives. Under these circumstances it can scarcely be denied that the experience has been an efficacious sign of conversion and therefore of reconciliation in the total human sense which is the experiential side of the coin of divine forgiveness.

What is common in all these instances is in the first place that, though not officially designated as one of the seven sacraments acknowledged since the twelfth century, the sign is efficacious. Secondly, what is common is that, because they are not officially designated, the sign (or sacrament in the broad sense) is not looked for in a special formula or ceremony but in the living relationships of the living members of the community that is Church. In other words the broadly sacramental character of the event is not dependent on jurisdiction, ordination, delegation or status. It depends on the charity, humility, honesty and welcome that the people involved express in their relationships with one another. It is the ministry of the healing forgiveness of God in Jesus Christ practiced in the immediacy of human experience, not in symbolic form once removed from ordinary experience.

A further common element in all these examples is that they do not begin with an examination of conscience for what should be repented and confessed. They begin with an intensified experience of the loving and welcoming presence of God mediated by the warm, simple and unpretentious ministry of Christians to one another. This, of course, is what we mean by speaking of the Church as the body, or bodily presence, of the risen Christ in the world. This is what we mean when we say that the Church as such is the basic sacrament of the presence and continuing action of God in Christ in the world. It is the living Church in its everyday life and relationships that is charged with the continuing task of reconciliation and conversion.

It is within this context that any formal rite of the sacrament of penance takes place. To the extent that the official sacrament is seen as continuous with the reconciliation process in the living Church, symbolizing and capping it and bringing it to a moment of solemnization in a community act of worship, the sacramental functioning of the three levels will be in place. What seems to be required is that either people approach the sacrament of penance because they have already had an intensified experience of the forgiving love of God in their lives which has brought them to an awareness of sinfulness and of the possibility and need of conversion, or the sacramental celebration must be such that it brings people by this route. Because the first can not be assumed when people are commanded to come according to the calendar, not according to their own experience, therefore the new forms of the rite try to supply the lack within the ceremony.

This is the logic underlying the mixed rite. It is also the purpose of the scripture reading in the reconciliation of individual penitents. Yet the time elapsing is really too short for personal assimilation and growth such as is supposed by the progression from deeper experience of the love of God to a clearer awareness both of sinfulness and of mercy. For this reason, the use of penitential services in which there is neither confession nor absolution seems to be more helpful, when the rite with general absolution can not be used. Such a penitential service, which is not designated as sacramental in the strict sense can, if well chosen and prepared and executed, create the environment of acceptance and welcome and community support which can set people on the road towards a further realization both of their own sinfulness and of the greater mercy of God that is always able to overcome it. People will travel that road at differing speeds and some will reach a point sooner or later where confession is a spontaneously felt need.

For those who never come to that point there is no way anymore in our pluralistic and critically alert society in which they can be compelled by physical, social or psychological force to make their confession. People are simply staying away in great numbers, and they are staying away because they do not find the sacrament meeting a spontaneously felt need. The only way to attract them back is to offer sacramental celebration in a way that meets the felt need. We are in fact in a situation which is in many ways parallel to the later patristic period when public or canonical penance was officially in force and in practice largely ignored. What happened then, as shown in earlier chapters, is that from the felt needs of the living Church new patterns emerged. This is clearly what is needed now.

For some, of course, the rite for the reconciliation of individual penitents, that is, individual confession, retains its power to move them to continuing conversion. These people are not confessing because they are commanded to do so, but because for them the sign really signifies and effects what it signifies. They experience the functioning of the sacrament at the three levels, or more accurately speaking they experience not only the ritual and the ritual assurances but the inner conversion also, and the latter points convincingly to the forgiveness of God. This may be because they have the advantage of being able to confess within the context of spiritual direction, but this will probably always be available only to the privileged few. Or it may be that though the encounters are few, brief and more or less anonymous, the sacrament is well ministered within a community in which reconciliation and conversion are in fact being ministered by many people in many relationships that constantly serve to build up a community vividly aware of

God's presence in its midst. It may even be that some find an efficacious sign of conversion in the sacrament because they themselves have grown to a personal maturity in the faith that asks for relatively little community support and reinforcement.

All of this perhaps begs for a clearer statement on the meaning of reconciliation and conversion. The question may occur to some readers whether people may not be badly deceived when making judgements that something does or does not mediate a conversion for them. People can, of course, delude themselves in the matter, on the basis of emotional enthusiasm or the flattery of others or a purely moralistic conception of what is involved in conversion to God. However, much as this possibility must be reckoned with, we are nevertheless obliged to make such judgements in our own lives. Official assurances can not substitute because either they are based upon our own experiences as we express them in our words and in our changed conduct or else they are irrelevant to the issue.

People judge conversion, grace and salvation in their lives on the kinds of experiences described in the beginning of this chapter. They find themselves confused, inhibited, frightened and unfree. They are brought to a point of recognition and acceptance of the truth of their relation to God and to other people (the *Shepherd* of Hermas has the angel of repentance say that true penance is deep understanding) and in this recognition and acceptance they feel liberated. An important question, of course, is whether they only feel liberated or whether their lives are liberated, that is, more free to be present to others, to minister to the needs of others, to be present to God in a certain unhassled simplicity, to accept their own dependency and limitations. In a slightly different perspective, they find initially that their lives are dissipated, disoriented, goalless or frantic. They are brought to a steady focus, a quiet sense of purpose, a growing sense of integration of all aspects and activities of their lives. The focus and integration endure. There is something to live for, something to make life worthwhile that is really worthy of their total dedication and they find a serenity that can encompass all untoward happenings. When people have experiences like these and they endure, there is a self-validating quality in them that gives clear assurance of being on a path of reconciliation and conversion, a path of grace leading to salvation.

One important factor in the efficacy of the sacrament of penance that appears quite commonly to be overlooked in our time is that of the works of penance imposed, the so-called satisfaction. In the earlier practice of the Church heavy emphasis was placed on the works of penance to be performed. In the system of canonical penance, actual confession of specific sins may not have taken place at all where the sin was known publicly or to the bishop. The *exomologesis* consisted of taking on the status of penitent, submitting to the discipline of the Church for reconciliations, and performing the prescribed works of penance. In the desert practice and in the monastic tradition, confession did take place in the context of manifestation of conscience, and was thought to be in itself salutary though also a way of obtaining appropriate counsel toward continuing conversion and the pursuit of perfection. In the tariff or private penance spread by the Celtic monks, the purpose of confession seems to have been only for the proper determination of the penance that should be done. In the conflict between the two systems, Theodulf and others insisted that while confession to a priest was good, so was confession to God alone. The assumption seemed to be that the penances would in any case be performed.

Since the twelfth century the emphasis in the sacrament has been on the confession rather than on the "satisfaction" This insight, drawn from the desert and monastic traditions originally, seems in many ways a helpful one. The root issue of repentance is surely to recognize and acknowledge oneself as a sinner before the exigent holiness of God. Moreover, it does not seem very effective or authentic to do this in generic terms without attempting a quite specific discernment of how that sinfulness shows itself in one's life, hence the usefulness of examination of conscience and more specific confession. It was quite certainly mistaken zeal to try to assign "proportionate" penances for particular sins, and no one really mourns the passing of the penitentials with all the problems they generated. Therefore, the shift to an emphasis on the healing force of humble confession and the recognition that repentance cannot be measured by time or severity of penances performed seems to be in continuity with the best insights and understanding that emerge from our tradition.

Nevertheless, Christian ascetical lore has maintained with equal force that genuine penance has an interior and an exterior aspect. That is to say, it consists of conversion of heart and conversion of life, and these are not really two different conversions nor even two consecutive phases of the same conversion but two simultaneous aspects of the same conversion. One of the ways one knows most clearly whether a conversion is real or only a matter of self-delusion is by the way it bears fruit in changing life-style, changing relationships and changing behavior. It would seem, therefore, that the emphasis can not be placed solely on the confession, as though that completed the turning to God.

There are probably four reasons for the relative neglect of the element of works of repentance. One is clearly the concern to repudiate the attempt to measure repentance by externals, a concern which is in the best tradition from the desert fathers. A second reason is probably discomfort with the conceptual model of expiation, satisfaction, punishment, retaliation or retributive justice, which seems to express too petty an image of God, a repugnance which is also in the best tradition. A third reason may be the impact that the theology and practice of indulgences had on the diminution of penances previously thought appropriate. A fourth reason is very probably concern on the part of confessors not to impose anything that might cause anxiety because the penitent is not clear what it means, or is afraid of not being able to perform it, or finds it burdensome in a way the confessor did not intend and could not have known.

All four reasons suggest a certain prudent reserve in refraining from imposing penances that are fanciful, artificial or complicated. But all four reasons put together do not alter the fact that conversion of life is the exterior aspect of conversion of heart, so that even the desert fathers with their conscientious objections to the scale of the canonical penances did not hesitate to expect very arduous expressions of conversion of life from their spiritual disciples and penitents. But for the desert fathers such asceticism looked forward rather than backward. It was concerned with the exigences of an arduous turning to God in a sinful history and not with a measure of compensation for sins committed in the past. On this model some modern manuals[5] on the new rite suggest that penances imposed should normally express the actual exigences of conversion much more explicitly than casual assignment of memorized prayers, but that this might best be done by enlisting the penitent's own suggestions of suitable works of repentance from which something could be assigned as the sacramental penance.

[5]*E.g.* Ralph Keifer and Frederick McManus, *The Rite of Penance: Commentaries, Vol. I. Understanding the Documents* (Washington, D.C.: Liturgical Conference, 1975).

Recommended Reading

Sean Fagan, *Has Sin Changed?* (see footnote 3).

Carra de Vaux Saint-Cyr, *et al, The Sacrament of Penance* (Paramus, N.J.: Paulist, 1966). Proceedings of a symposium on history, theology and pastoral aspects.

Edward Schillebeeckx *ed., Sacramental Reconciliation* (N.Y.: Herder, 1971). Besides the essays mentioned in the previous chapter there are several pertaining to the matter of this chapter.

Ralph Keifer & Frederick McManus, *Rite of Penance* (see footnote 5).

CHAPTER VII

GRACE, SATISFACTION AND THE PROBLEM OF INDULGENCES

The question of "satisfaction", that is of suitable and "adequate" works of penance is evidently one which preoccupied the Church at each stage of the development of the rites, as will have been evident from Chapters III, IV and V. It was taken seriously in the ancient rites of public or canonical penance, it was critically re-evaluated in the desert practice, it inspired the elaborate tariffs of the penitentials, it provided one aspect of the conflict between the public and private penance traditions, and it underlies the practice of granting indulgences as well as the many disputes that arose over the practice of granting indulgences in the course of the centuries. As already suggested in Chapters V and VI, there are several issues involved in the question: what is adequate and suitable satisfaction? The problem of indulgences involves them all. For this reason, and because the practice has at various times been a cause of so much scandal and misunderstanding, some explicit reflection on the history and meaning of indulgences seems to be in order.

The questions that must be confronted seem to be as follows. If salvation (and conversion, therefore) is by the grace, the utterly gratuitous gift, of God, what is the role of human freedom in it? As already indicated, the Catholic answer to this, experienced, meditated and critically evaluated through the ages, is that conversion is wholly the work of God's grace but at the same time wholly the response of human freedom. The grace of God does not crush human freedom nor substitute for it. Rather it enables, empowers, liberates human freedom from what is merely potential to what is actual. The second question that necessarily arises is how the human response is expressed. Here the Catholic answer has been emphatic. The response is more than an inner turning of the heart in acknowledgement of one's own sinfulness and dependence on God's grace and in an act of faith in Jesus as the salvation of God. The response is a total turning of one's life in all its relationships and activities and in all its dimensions. Indeed it is necessarily a community response because it involves all relationships, activities and dimensions of human life. The response, therefore, is arduous. It means changes in behavior and attitudes that are not easily made, retrenchments in various ways from patterns of self-indulgence and self-assertion, bold efforts in other ways to move beyond patterns of cowardice and laziness and failure of compassion. In the traditional practice and theory there has always been a sense that these practical changes should be sustained, fostered, and reinforced by going beyond the obviously necessary changes in behavior. Hence the traditional insistence on the necessity of prayer, fasting and almsdeeds,which could also be described somewhat more broadly as prayer, self-denial and charity.

The third question that arises in a Catholic context, then, is what difference the sacraments make in this event of conversion. As related in the earlier chapters, there can be no question of a claim that they so change the nature of the conversion that the human element is no longer necessary. The sacramental grace, in other words, does not substitute for the inner turning of the heart nor yet for the outer turning of behavior and relationships and total life-style. The earlier practices of the rites of penance stressed the works of repentance and focused on confession of sin only as the entry into the status of penitent and the basis for determining the works of penance that were appropriate. They focused on the reconciliation as the conclusion of the period of penance in which the works of penance were performed. Indeed, one might conclude from the recurring mediaeval assertion that confession to a priest is good but confession to God alone is good too, that there has been some hesitancy in the past to give any efficacy to the sacramental rite other than its practical helpfulness in fostering true conversion concretely expressed.[1] Stated positively, the Catholic position seems to be that the institutional Church administers and insists upon this sacramental rite because it is convinced that its members need such official, corporate, liturgical mediation of the grace of conversion, and because it is therefore also convinced that Jesus himself, alive in his Church by the Resurrection and by his Spirit, intends the ministry of reconciliation entrusted to the Church to be exercised in this way.

It would seem, then, that the efficacy of the sacrament is in bringing people to true repentance, interior and exterior, so that it supports them in works of penance. The early history certainly endorses this understanding both in the canonical penance practice and in that of private penance in the Celtic and English churches. Yet there are also indications that gradually the Church was seen as substituting or supplying for some or all of the works of penance seen as inherently necessary or appropriate on the part of the penitent. The intervention of the martyrs and confessors of the faith is an early example of this. By their merits and pleas penitents were reconciled without having to complete the full canonical penance that had been prescribed, apparently because vicarious penance had been done for them by the martyrs.[2] Likewise, the prayer and lamentation of the bishop and congregation on behalf of the penitents was apparently deemed to have lightened their obligation of penance, as was the confessor's sharing of the penance in the

---

[1]See discussion of this in Chapter V. Assertions previously documented are repeated in this chapter without further footnotes.

[2]See Bernhard Poschmann, *Penance and the Anointing of the Sick* (N.Y.: Herder, 1964), pp. 75-80.

private penance tradition. In the tariff penance of the penitentials, the practice of "redemptions" (or substitution of
something more readily feasible) in fact lightened the
penance, sometimes by substituting prayer for fasting.
Besides this there is an interesting history of so-called "abso-
lutions" (intercessory prayers for forgiveness deemed of
themselves efficacious because recited by holders of "the
power of the keys") which became important in the eleventh
century when reconciliation generally began to be granted
before the conclusion of the penance. Though they were at
that time already incorporated into the sacramental rite
itself, it seems that they also continued to be pronounced
separately. It was apparently understood that such absolu-
tions effected some remission of punishment by God himself
which was thought to be due.[3]

A new situation arose with the appearance of indulgences
in the strict sense of the term. Scattered instances are
recorded from the eleventh century and the Fourth Lateran
Council of 1215 already found it necessary to warn against
abuses — abuses which had long passed all tolerable bounds
before the Protestant Reformation of the sixteenth century
challenged them and the Council of Trent tried to restrain
them by putting indulgences in theological context.[4] The
indulgences were acts of jurisdiction by ecclesiastical
authority remitting ecclesiastical penances upon performance of acts of piety or charity, usually pilgrimages to
certain churches or the giving of alms. They might be reduc-
tions or total remissions. The grant of the indulgences
claimed without qualification the authority to remit the
ecclesiastical penance, and it carried the prayer and the hope
that this would be effective in the eyes of God to release the
penitent from divine punishment.

From the twelfth century onwards anxiety is expressed by
theologians over the meaning of such indulgences. There is a
general sense that unless there is a genuine conversion, such

[3]*Ibid.*, pp. 210-215.
[4]*Ibid.*, pp. 215-232.

remission of penance cannot mean anything in the eyes of God. Eventually it was agreed, however, that indulgences must remit "the pains of purgatory", otherwise there would have been no good reason to grant them, for the beneficiaries would be the worse for them in the end.[5] From this, almost imperceptibly, comes the tacit understanding that the "power of the keys" extends to jurisdiction over the "punishment of purgatory", that is, that it covers the penitent's relationship to God beyond death — a relationship and outcome which previous generations had always simply committed to the mercy of God. The justification for such a claim to jurisdiction was found in the understanding that the merits of the passion of Christ and of the deaths of the martyrs had been entrusted to the Church as a "treasury" to be dispensed to those in need. It was, in fact, no longer based on the sacramental efficacy of the sacrament of penance but simply on the power of jurisdiction of pope and bishops, from which other priests, even parish priests acting as confessors, were excluded.

The separation from sacramental penance raised in even more acute form the question as to how the granting of an indulgence affected the penitent's need to do penance personally and whether it was dependent on the penitent's willingness to do penance personally. Disagreement on this question continued for centuries.[6] This question became urgent with the claim to apply or to grant indulgences in favor of the dead in consideration of enlistment in a crusade or monetary contribution to the building of certain churches by the living. Eventually official church statements defended the practice against Luther.[7] In any case, although much remained unresolved in the theological explanation of the practice of granting indulgences, the official teaching of the Church vigorously defended the practice at the Council

[5] This is the theological development according to Poschmann's interpretation. *op. cit.*, pp. 219-223. Cf. also Karl Rahner, "Indulgences", in *Sacramentum Mundi*, ed. Karl Rahner *et al.* (N.Y.: Herder, 1969) Vol. 3, pp. 123-129.

[6] Poschmann, *op. cit.*, pp. 226-227.

[7] Details given in *ibid.*, pp. 227-229.

of Trent and in the Code of Canon Law promulgated in 1918.[8] Because indulgences continue to be granted, it seems to be necessary to discover in the practice and in the traditional teaching those elements of enduring value and meaning that can be formulated in terms intelligible within a contemporary perception of reality.

The definition of an indulgence that remains official to this time is that it is a "remission before God of the temporal punishment due to sins whose guilt has been forgiven" and that an indulgence is conceded by Church authority "from the Church's treasury for the living by means of absolution, and for the dead by means of intercession".[9] The understanding of the practice obviously depends heavily in this definition on the understanding of the notion of "temporal punishment due to sins whose guilt has been forgiven". The distinction between "guilt" and "punishment due" was made official Church teaching by the Council of Trent.[10] Though not officially defined, this distinction seems to be concerned with the obvious truth that a radical change of heart or attitude necessarily means reconciliation with God or "justification" and yet leaves much to be put right.

The "punishment due" or "temporal punishment" as it is sometimes designated need not be understood in a vindictive or arbitrarily retributive sense. In other words, it is not necessary to imagine God as inventing punishments to inflict on sinners. The "punishments" are simply the consequences of lives, actions, relationships, goals and criteria that have been disoriented, out of focus from the only perspective that is adequate and can make sense of human existence. Even when there is an inner turning back, the reorienting of the whole of human existence cannot usually be instantaneous. It involves certain patterns of comple-

---

[8]For full list of official pronouncements see Rahner, *op. cit.,* pp. 123-124, or Poschmann, *op. cit.,* pp. 229-230. For key texts in translation, see J. Neuner and H. Roos, *The Teaching of the Catholic Church* (N.Y.: Alba House, 1967, pp. 325-330.

[9]*C.I.C.* (1918), C. 911. Translation taken from Neuner and Roos, *op. cit.,* p. 330.

[10]See footnote 8.

mentarity with others, habits hard to change, actual dispositions of material goods, power, privilege and obligations. It involves structures of society. It also involves personal dispositions, inclinations, perceptions, expectations and attitudes. The sinfulness in all of these may not be at all evident even to the sincerely penitent, and when and where it becomes evident it may not be at all easy to change the patterns. The burden of dealing with such residues of sin seems to be a more reasonable way to envisage the "temporal punishment due when guilt is forgiven" than the notion that a certain commensurate amount of pain or hardship is inflicted as arbitrary punishment of sin in order to appease the justice of God.

If the punishment due for sin is seen in this way, then the central concern of works of penance is to discern and put right what has been distorted. And in this case, the adequate and appropriate "works of penance" will usually not be essentially or primarily imposed penances such as were the canonical penances of the ancient Church or the tariff penances of the mediaeval Church. The adequate and appropriate penance then really becomes a matter for a continuing quest for discernment and for fidelity to the conversion as its implications unfold further. The role of the imposed penance and of the authority that imposes it, then, can only be subsidiary to the essential penance. That is to say, its function is necessarily to help the penitent make the discernment and grow to fuller fidelity to the conversion. Prayer obviously fosters such discernment and fidelity, especially when it is not an arbitrary and repetitious recital but is appropriate to the particular situation. Equally obviously, practices of self-denial will tend to dispose a person favorably to such discernment and fidelity, and the cumulative wisdom of the tradition identifies fasting as the basic or central practice of self-denial that is apt to do this. Finally, and perhaps most obviously of all, charity, the practical exercise of concern for the needs of others, disposes to fuller realization of conversion because it goes directly to the heart of the problem both of sin and of the consequences of sin (or punishment due), namely the disorientation in which community and communion fall apart and persons become isolated competitors.

Insofar as indulgences originally "forgave" or excused from elaborate and lengthy canonical or tariff penances in favor of works of piety having a community significance like the building of a church and (however ill-advisedly) the fighting of a crusade, it is quite easy to understand that the intervention of the Church as communion lightens the burden of the extrinsic or imposed penances by which a penitent might be led to clearer understanding and more generous implementation of all that was essentially involved in the repentance. From the essential works of penance, that is, the turning from sin to God and putting right what can be mended, the Church could of course in no way excuse. In our times, however, the excusing of the canonical or tariff penance can be no more than a fiction because such penances are no longer in use. Yet the claim remains that there is a "remission before God of the temporal punishment due". This claim certainly cannot intend something more than is claimed for the sacrament of penance.[11] The claim for the sacrament of penance is that it mediates reconciliation with God not by by-passing personal conversion but by fostering it. In the same way, it seems to be the sense of the claim being made for the practice of granting indulgences that they mediate reconciliation with God in further and progressive ways after the initial conversion by facilitating or fostering the necessary works of repentance which make the inner turning to God effective in all aspects of life in the world among other people.

One may ask at this point whether it is possible to understand more clearly how such an influence might work. Minimally, certainly, the granting of an indulgence simply underscores what is happening all the time, namely that the saving grace of Christ's redemptive death and resurrection

---

[11]*Cf.* Rahner, *op. cit.*, pp. 123-124, and "Punishment of Sins", *ibid.*, Vol. 6, pp. 92-94.

anticipates and welcomes our conversion at every step of the way, making that which is in itself impossible not only possible but a joyful task and a light burden. The indulgence serves as a reminder and a constant insistence on this, and as such it offers encouragement. Beyond this, the granting of an indulgence offers an immediate and specific incentive and goal, and therefore coaxes people along, one step at a time. Therefore it functions as an opening of the "treasury of the Church" inasmuch as the proclamation of indulgence elicits the readiness of recipients to respond and avail themselves of what is in fact always there for them. At the lowest level one may suppose that people respond because they sense they are being offered "a bargain". In many cases indulgences are also effective in bringing about the continuing repentance which they signify because they have a strong community dimension, as with pilgrimages and novenas and other occasions that bring large numbers of people together in a spirit of prayerfulness and deeper awareness of God's caring for them and God's call to them. The sense of Christian community and common purpose in Christ that is fostered is evidently so efficacious for continuing conversion in the encouragement, assurance and challenge that it offers, that it is probably more effective for most people than a great deal of imposed penance.

However, precisely because indulgences emphasize the anticipatory grace of God extended to us in Christ, and because they appear as "bargains", and because they offer a certain exhilarating sense of community support, it is really necessary that they be presented in ways that do not suggest that they can substitute for the essential conversion of life and behavior. While many Catholics today think of their destiny in or beyond death as mystery hidden in the inscrutable designs of God, others think of heaven, hell and purgatory in very concrete terms. The granting of indulgences with reference to time, like "seven years and seven quarantines", logical enough when indulgences actually remitted canonical penances imposed by the Church, is still erroneously understood by some Catholics as a claim to shorten temporal extension of punishment envisaged as stretching through a quasi-time "after" death. This is more than an academic mistake concerning the original reference of the time specifications. It carries with it the implication that an indulgence can substitute for the essential penance, an implication that vitiates the whole purpose of the granting of indulgences which is to facilitate and encourage continuing and full conversion.

Such a misunderstanding could be devastating in any sphere of Christian life but it seems particularly destructive in the area of social justice and reconstruction of true community in the human family. Any inner turning back to God carries implications not only for relationships with individuals and face to face groups like the immediate family and the people in one's daily work situation, but also for the whole network of relationships that make up the structures of our society. We tend to take much of this network totally for granted as though we had been dropped into "slots" in society and could do only what has been foreordained as the proper behavior in the slot. No matter how much that behavior may oppress other people or exclude them or define them as enemies through no fault of their own, it is difficult for us to accept responsibility for the sinfulness of the relationships because they are part of the pattern of our society and therefore are taken for granted. For this reason one has to be rather constantly alert and "tuned in" to the divine call to conversion of the whole complex of the disoriented human situation in order even to discern what is out of focus. Beyond that, one has to be constantly challenged and instructed to accept responsibility for what seems quite beyond the control of any individual and therefore is easily assumed to be beyond the control of all individuals.

Any suggestion that penance stops with the inner conversion of the heart is really a betrayal of the gospel of Christ which has to do with the redemption of the world and therefore with the conversion of society as well as individuals and with the conversion of individuals in all dimensions of their lives. The misunderstanding of indulgences is certainly one such suggestion that one can be excused from the practical implications of conversion in the many dimensions of life by an ecclesiastical sanction that cancels the obligation in the sight of God. A truer understanding, on the other hand, could be very helpful. It would foster an awareness that we really need the continuing support of the Christian community alive with the Spirit of the risen Christ in order to implement a continuing conversion in all dimensions of our lives. Moreover, it would constantly draw attention to the need for such implementation even after confession of sin and inner conversion and absolution — a need that may not be evident enough from the ritual of sacramental penance unless the participants are personally alert to it.

A truer understanding of indulgences should certainly foster an awareness that real conversion, generally (if always only partially) implemented in the various dimensions of life, is essentially a community response involving mutual support, reciprocal challenge, joint endeavor. It is essentially a community response because the most basic issue is the quality of relationships, of empathy practically expressed, of sensitivity to the needs and existence of others. The most basic issue is the call to be for God and for others, with God and with others, in God and in others in the context of a wounded world, a broken history, a network of human relations weakened and complicated by resentments, distrust, injustices, hatreds and exclusions. Even with the grace of God the repairing of relationships cannot be the task of individuals striving in isolation to accomplish the work of repentance in their lives.

The sense of indulgences, properly understood, is probably most cogently and completely recognized where there is the strongest and most practically concrete sense of sin and sinfulness. Yet the reverse is also true, namely that the practice of granting and gaining indulgences can foster a keener awareness and a more authentic discernment of sinfulness and of the residues of sin in structures, expectations, relationships and attitudes.

Recommended Reading

Bernhard Poschmann, *Penance and the Anointing of the Sick*. (N.Y.: Herder, 1964).

Karl Rahner, "Remarks on the Theology of Indulgences", *Theological Investigations,* Vol. II, (Baltimore: Helicon, 1963), pp. 175-202.

CHAPTER VIII

THE MINISTRY OF THE SACRAMENT: THE ROLE OF CONFESSOR

Most of what will be said in this chapter applies to the lady with the welcoming coffee pot as much as to the ordained priest with faculties to absolve in the name of the Church. Canonical matters such as faculties, censures, reserved sins, are not dealt with in this volume. Theologically and pastorally, the difference in the function of the ordained priest is that he ministers an official sacrament of the Church on behalf of the institutional Church and strictly under the conditions and rules set by the institutional Church. All Christians, including ordained priests, are called to *be* sacraments of reconciliation to one another and to the world (in the broader sense of sacrament). That means that they are called to minister to others by mediating reconciliation and conversion whenever they can.

This is done in many ways — by prayer, by suffering injuries without revenge and forgiving offenses against oneself, by friendship and community bonds, by counsel and encouragement and admonition. However, this ministry also frequently calls on individual Christians to receive from others confessions of failure, sinfulness, specific sins, shame, discouragement and temptations. It calls on them to receive such confessions in the charity of Christ and to respond to them with the heart of Christ on behalf of the whole body of Christ which is the Church, the community of the faithful which is the living Church. This is a mediation of grace at the grassroots of the redemption going on in the world. It is a mediation of grace by wounded healers. It must be characterized by exigence and honesty, but it can never be in any way condescending because all are involved in the same sinfulness and the same struggle.

Since the counter-Reformation and Catholic reform of the sixteenth century, a fairly extensive literature has accumulated on the role of the confessor, such as the writings of Francis de Sales and Alphonsus Liguori. There is also no lack of role models, such as Philip Neri and Jean Vianney. Yet it may be well to reflect on the role and tasks and qualities of the confessor in terms of the needs of the Christian community in our own time.

There has been some polarity in the past as to whether the confessor in the sacrament in the strict sense should maintain a careful psychological distance and play an impersonal, official role, keeping his own emotions and affections carefully out of the relationship with penitents so as to ensure that the sacrament is as fully as possible the action of Christ and not of another, and so as to encourage the penitent to relate directly to Christ and not to another. This option would seem to be the logical one if the role of confessor is seen primarily as a judicial role and the Church in whose name he speaks and acts primarily or exclusively as institution. The other possibility is that the confessor should precisely make it his business to be and to act as a friend of his penitents, to get his emotions involved in the relationships, cultivating affection for them and winning their affection for him. This option would seem to be the better one if sacramentality is understood as described in Chapter VI, in terms of the charity and life of the whole Church as the mediation of the grace of Christ and therefore as the matrix within which particular sacramental celebrations take on their meaning.

In our past traditions there is a very strong pressure to keep the priest confessor in a paternal role, even though that role may be played affectionately rather than with aloofness. The origin of this is clear. In the desert and in the monastic tradition it was the role of elders, senior both in age and in experience. When the custom first spread beyond the monasteries to the laity, it appears that confessions were frequently made to abbots, who were cast in the paternal role already by virtue of their office. As the traditions of the sacrament of penance have come down to us in modern times, it was not strange that this pattern should be retained, because priests in most countries were commonly addressed as "Father" no matter how young and inexperienced they might be nor how old or experienced might be the lay persons with whom they were in conversation. Besides, they were expected to be the theological and spiritual experts and were expected to administer the sacraments and dispense advice from their book learning

In present circumstances, this places an intolerable burden on many priests, especially younger diocesan priests who are ordained when very young and often extremely inexperienced. It would have been a burden at any time, but it is aggravated in our times because priests are no longer significantly better educated than their congregations in many places and because the study of theology, scripture, spirituality and liturgy are wide open to the laity so that the priest is not always the expert in these fields in encounters with the laity. Moreover, most people today do not value book learning above experience in a situation such as the sacrament of penance and a relationship in which they seek guidance in a continuing Christian conversion. They look for someone who understands their situation from his own experience of wrestling with it.

Under these circumstances it is probably more constructive to see the role of the priest in general and the role of the confessor and spiritual director in particular as a fraternal rather than paternal role. This is certainly the way this ministry is successfully discharged by lay people acting outside the sacramental framework in the strict sense. These lay and unofficial ministers of reconciliation and conversion have no reason to assume a role that is in any way superior or condescending to those who approach them for help. They can only respond as sister and brother sharing the struggle and the responsibility and the prayer and also the sinfulness of the community. But in our society it is precisely this kind of relationship among peers that is sought for strength and support because it offers promise of greater and more intimate understanding based on common experience.

To relate in a brotherly or sisterly way is also, of course, to make oneself more vulnerable, more accessible, more subject to comparison and challenge, more easily put on the spot, less easily able to hide one's person behind the role and function. It is in fact closer to the ministry of the historical Jesus and the Apostles and earliest leaders of the Christian community who would not claim titles or special privilege. In the sisterly or brotherly role one must stand before others in the simplicity and poverty of one's own being, and therefore one must minister out of one's own poverty and weakness and not out of the strength of an institutional status. And this is the example that Jesus gave us, the power of God mediated in human weakness, which has an appeal for conversion of hearts and lives that the use of human power and status does not have. But apart from the appeal that it has for others, the sisterly or brotherly role is easier for the one who plays it because it does not demand perfection, spiritual eminence, inerrancy or great wisdom; it really only demands humility and compassion and vulnerability.

The tasks of the confessor are basically five: to pray with and for the penitent; to listen with deep compassion on behalf of God and the community; to discern the spiritual situation of the penitent from what the latter has freely revealed (and perhaps gently to educate the conscience of the penitent); to convey the forgiveness of God; and to express the exigence of God's call to conversion. It may be helpful to consider each of these in turn.

The first task is not really to receive the confession, but to pray. There is a dogged consistency on this point in the tradition. The bishop in the ancient canonical penance is to meet the penitents, weep and lament with them and pray over them. The desert elders pray for their charges before they go out to meet them or seek them and they pray again with them when they encounter them. The purpose of the prayer is evidently to "tune in to God" more intently so as to be able to discern his word to this particular disciple. This carries over into the monastic tradition. The *pseudo-Roman Penitential* instructs the priest that when he sees a penitent approaching he must first quickly disappear into a private room or corner to recite a preliminary prayer. The text of the prayer is one of personal humility and contrition for the priest's own sins and a petition to be able to help the other out of his own utter unworthiness. Theodulf is willing to admit that it is useful to confess to priests mainly because this involves the exchange of prayers.[1] Moreover, down to the present time the exhortations are steadily repeated to pray in deep humility realizing one's own sinfulness and one's great need to be about the business of one's own conversion while hoping with the grace of God to mediate conversion for others, to pray then for and with the penitent.

It is clear that this is the teaching of the tradition and one would need no further reason for following it. Yet it is tempting to conjecture why all those with the experience of mediating conversions for others have concluded so emphatically that this is the first task. Certainly, they are concerned with the need to acknowledge one's own sinfulness so that the relationship can be honest and based on respect for the other. It is also evident, that they give the exhortation to pray for enlightenment so that good discernments may be made. But beyond this, it would seem to be prompted by the realization that none of us converts sinners but God, and that God alone forgives so that our role is to beg that forgiveness from Him for ourselves and for others.

---

[1] References are not given here because all the examples are drawn from the earlier, historical chapters in which the references are given in detail.

There may be one other reason: the relationship between confessor and penitent acquires a different character when they pray together.

The second task is to listen on behalf of God and the Christian community and to receive the confession in compassion. It is a task of mourning with a mourner, not of conducting a cross-examination. From the penitent's point of view the transforming aspect is first and foremost the recognition and acknowledgement of oneself as a sinner, and then the specific acknowledgement of the pattern of sinfulness that holds sway in one's life, and finally particular actions or problems in which it manifests itself, though the chronology of the prior examination of conscience probably moved in the opposite direction. But because the transforming power of the confession tends to be in the pattern in which the essential *exomologesis* lies in putting oneself metaphorically in the rank of penitent, a general avowal of sinfulness is not a preliminary but ought to be received with serious attention as central content of the confession.[2]

Most people find it quite hard to receive a confession from another, possibly particularly so in our culture where we are taught to think no negative thoughts about ourselves and where it therefore seems a little morbid to humble oneself before another with admissions of wrongdoing, guilt, shame, hateful attitudes and humiliating weaknesses. It is most threatening and most difficult to receive a confession from another when the other is most like oneself in age, sex and situation. To receive a confession from another with genuine compassion one ought to have confronted one's own sinfulness as explicitly and honestly as possible in the context of a vivid awareness of the mercy of God. In any case, it is easier to receive a confession in an authentic, fully human and vulnerable way in a sisterly or brotherly role

[2]This principle is clear in the ancient practice, but for the insight that this is the logic of the practices of *exomologesis* I am indebted to conversational remarks of Thomas E. Clarke, S.J. of the Woodstock Center for Theological Reflection at Georgetown University. The same point is made by contemporary Protestant writer Richard Foster, *Celebration of Discipline* (N.Y.: Harper, 1978), Chapter 10.

than in a maternal or paternal role.

The receiving of the confession, of course, demands a response which has to be made in reliance on the Holy Spirit and not on one's own wisdom, learning, psychological sophistication or other human skill, because one is putting oneself at the disposal of God to mediate God's response to the penitent. Many saintly and experienced people have suggested that it is far better to say little or nothing in response than to risk introducing static on God's line to this penitent out of personal enthusiasm for giving lots of advice and solving other people's problems for them. There is one message that must always be given: God is merciful and welcomes sinners; access to the Reign of God is on the basis of need and not of personal stores of virtue or unblemished records; repentance is possible in the first place because he has already extended his welcome and made our repentance possible; he guides into the right paths all who pray and listen for his word.

There is another way to make a response that is not dominating or interfering and that is by a humble personal witness out of one's own life and prayer. In such a fraternal or sisterly testimony one does not claim to speak for God or to interpret God's word to the other, much less to tell the other what to do in his or her life. One simply offers witness, testimony out of one's own life as a gift laid down quietly on the table quite unaggressively so that it can be picked up or left there. Many people are embarrassed to do this. They do not want to be more personal than is necessary nor to expose themselves in this way. But especially in the case of a penitent who is going to return one or more times, perhaps regularly, an appropriate personal witness in which one exposes oneself a bit in a relevant and non-distracting way is a great help to the other in being more personal, direct and simple about his or her confessions.

Sometimes there is an unmistakable need to educate the conscience of the other. All the available sources in the tradition seem to be agreed that one should approach this with the greatest humility about one's own blind spots, the greatest respect for the freedom and dignity of the other, and a reverential fear of trying to hurry God's dealings with another person.

The fourth task of the confessor is to be the living expression of God's forgiveness, either by official absolution in the name of the institutional Church or personal warmth and welcome. Some lay persons who regularly mediate unofficial reconciliation and conversion have adopted symbolic modes of expression in gesture and word. A number of Protestant testimonies concerning this are available.[3]

The final and very delicate task of the confessor is to express with great love and compassion and personal humility the exigence of God's call to conversion which means not only the inner conversion of the heart but the outer conversion of life, which means works of repentance. On this we have very explicit testimony and very helpful indications from the desert fathers and the monastic traditions.[4] The main points seem to be the following. One must express the exigence of God's love which demands a total return, a turning of one's heart and steps, and which does not tolerate the enshrining of idols side by side with the true God. However, there is no question of retribution or revenge, only of discerning what it takes to turn and retrace one's steps to come home to the Father's house. Moreover, God's time is good time not frantic time; it is growing time not crash-production time; it is desert time, camel time, not city automobile speed. Besides this, it is a gentle turning, not a gymnastic caper; it is better attained by little attention to fancy invented penances and by assiduous attention to the steps of repentance that the providence of God lays out in the circumstances of daily life. Finally, when one sends another off on a path of repentance one must accompany him or her at least a substantial part of the way, fast for fast, vigil for vigil. The desert fathers' custom seemed to be to go all the way with the penitent. The rule for priests in the

---

[3]*ibid.*

[4]It may be worth while to turn back to Chapter III and its footnotes at this point.

pseudo-Roman Penitential was to accompany the penitent in his fast for at least a week or two, longer if possible. From these traditional indications of the tasks of the confessor, one might deduce easily enough the qualities to be sought and cultivated for this ministry. They certainly include humility, prayerfulness and the virtue of penitence, and beyond that, patience, sensitivity to people's verbal and non-verbal communication, gentleness, courage, affection, generosity and great docility to the Holy Spirit.

Recommended Reading

Kenneth Leech, *Soul Friend: A Study of Spirituality:* (London: Sheldon, 1977). This book by an Anglican is largely concerned with the role of the spiritual director and incidentally with that of the confessor.

Nathan Mitchell, ed., *The Rite of Penance: Commentaries, Vol. III. Background and Directions.* (Washington, D.C.: Liturgical Conference, 1978). The essay by Raymond Studzinski, "The Minister of Reconciliation: Some Historical Models" is particularly pertinent here.

Carra de Vaux Saint Cyr, ed. *The Sacrament of Penance,* (Paramus, N.J.: Paulist, 1966). This contains good essays on the Oriental Church and the Protestant traditions.

CHAPTER IX

THE WORLDLY DIMENSION: RECONCILIATION AND SOCIAL JUSTICE

What was written in Chapter VI about the efficacy of the sacrament in terms of personal reconciliation and conversion, and what was written in Chapter VIII about the role of the confessor, do not exhaust the description of the Christian ministry of reconciliation. Reconciliation as the total task of the Church, synonymous with redemption, is concerned with worldly as well as personal dimensions. It is concerned with the restoration of social structures in Christ because social structures are a dimension of human existence, and spirituality can not be divorced from our responsibility for one another even in the large structures of the public realm.[1] Inasmuch as the whole Church is the sacrament of reconciliation and conversion, the whole social justice question is part of the theme. But since this volume is concerned more particularly with the sacrament of penance in the strict sense, the real concern of the chapter is to establish the relationship between the sacrament strictly so-called and the practical issues of social justice in the society.

[1] For a full treatment of this thesis, see Thomas E. Clarke, S.J. ed *Above Every Name: The Lordship of Christ and Social Structures* (Ramsey, N.J.: Paulist Press, 1980).

The practice of individual confession has become such a problem both from the point of view of the penitent and from that of the confessor largely because of puzzlement over the nature of sin. The new form of the rite does nothing to assuage this unease over the authenticity of the sacramental confession, simply because it demands far more personal involvement and far more genuine discernment than the pre-Vatican II form really demanded. This pervasive problem with the sacrament in its most readily available form, is frequently interpreted as an unmitigated disaster — a situation from which one must recover so as to return to normalcy.[2] However, it may be more appropriate to regard the present situation as a crisis in the strict sense of that word —a situation calling for discernment, decision and new moves.

As explained in the Introduction and in Chapter I, there is indeed a crisis in the understanding of sin and sinfulness, but it is not a simple loss of the sense of sin. It is rather a questioning of some of the categories and perceptions of sin which have been current in the Catholic Church in recent generations. Committed Catholic believers, truly striving to live their lives in response to the gospel, as well as marginal Church members who have never reflected much on what it means to be a Christian, experience persistent problems with individual confession as they have known it. They have problems with the itemization and specification, and more particularly with the definition of sin in terms of culpability, that is to say in terms of the degree of freedom and deliberation involved. Moreover, they question the meaningfulness of repeated listings of these transgressions in the context of what appears as a wiping clean of the slate knowing it will presently be covered again with much the same list.

---

[2]Indeed the 1983 report on Penance and Reconciliation of the International Theological Commission, prepared for the 1983 world Synod of Bishops, even argues strongly for a return to the post-Tridentine discipline of the sacrament of Penance, and seems to worry that even a very restricted use of the second and third forms of the present rite is corrupting the Catholic people. See *Penance and Reconciliation*, B.IV.c. and C. II. 4. (which can be found in *Origins*, N.C. Documentary Service, Vol. 13, no.31, January 12, 1984, pp 520-522.)

This kind of crisis of conscience is much more symptomatic of a new growth towards maturity than of corruption
or decline. The autobiographies of great saints and mystics
such as Catharine of Siena, Ignatius of Loyola and Teresa of
Avila are enough to confirm this, if we are afraid to trust our
own experience. People are searching for more authenticity
in their relationship to God, just as they are aware of the
need for greater authenticity in their relationships with one
another. Even those who do not read contemporary theology find themselves keenly aware that any understanding of
grace and of redemption which does not manifest itself in
life experience must be inauthentic because it bypasses
human freedom. But for many people this remains inarticu-
late, vaguely surmised. In any case, there is certainly a
diffuse and persistent awareness of the need of redemption
in the modern world, and people are searching for the
definition and interpretation of this awareness.

It would seem to be at this juncture that the sacrament of
penance as a repeated act and as an individual act can begin
to make sense. Inasmuch as it is a more specific mediation of
conversion, it certainly ought to be a continuing exercise of
discernment in the particular circumstances of a believer's
life. Present directives to include scripture reading and
reflection upon it in the celebration of the individual rite of
reconciliation, seem to open the way for precisely such
ongoing practice of discernment. All of scripture seems to
suggest that the discernment of sin and of sinfulness arises
out of the experience of suffering, articulated and interpreted in the light of growing awareness of the indiscrimi-
nate, passionate, boundlessly creative love of God. It would
seem that a continuing conversion must somehow happen
after this pattern, so that the mediation of continuing conversion should foster this kind of awareness and reflection.

The discovery of sinfulness, of disorientation, by reflection on suffering in the light of God's love can and must, of
course, have reference to the private lives of the individuals
concerned. But it can never have reference only to those
private lives, because the reality of sin and suffering is not
circumscribed in that way. This realization seems to come

more easily to the poor and the oppressed. That, of coure, is why some theologians recently have written of the "hermeneutic privilege" of the poor with respect to the gospel.[3] Yet it is obviously just as important for those of us who are not poor and oppressed to grow to a keener and more reflective understanding of the inter-personal and public, structural dimensions of sin and redemption. The question arises, therefore, as to how the sacrament of penance can foster this growth.

People seem to be converted more deeply not by rational argument but by radicalizing experiences, and experiences seem to be radicalizing for some people in a way that they are not for others. At the heart of the process of any conversion is a kind of openness or vulnerability to experience —an openness to be hurt by experiences but also to be changed by them and to have one's vision and goals and self-image changed by them. A conversion seems to hinge upon the reshaping of the imagination. In the experience of most people there is a tendency to see the world in terms of "our side" and "their side," in terms of the good and decent people to whom we belong and those untrustworthy and undeserving people who are outside the ranks to which we belong. It is a theme to which the preaching of Jesus constantly returns, not to endorse but to overturn it. Jesus evidently saw this struggle between inclusive and exclusive ways of building human community as central to human conversion and inseparable from the turning to God.

All this, of course, has always been true and all the great saints and mystics and teachers of the Christian tradition have been aware of it. The Christian story sparkles with a galaxy of names of those who in their continuing conversion to God found themselves becoming socially and politically more and more radical — always too radical for their times. One thinks immediately of Paul among the Corinthian con-

[3]For a survey and evaluation of literature on this topic, see M.K. Hellwig, "Good news for the poor: do they understand it better?" in *Tracing the Spirit*, ed. James E. Hug, S.J. (N.Y.: Paulist, 1983), pp.122 - 148. For a detailed explanation of the meaning of the claim, see Lee Cormie, "The Hermeneutical Privilege of the Oppressed," in *C.T.S.A. Proceedings*, Vol. 33, 1978, pp. 163-167.

verts, of Ambrose when chosen bishop, of the dying Augustine in his besieged city, of Francis of Assisi, of Dominic leaving the splendor of the bishops' expedition against the Albigensians, of Ignatius of Loyola, of a magnificent procession of Christian queens and noblewomen... The basic thrust of this conversion to God which is at the same time a conversion to the excluded fellow human beings, is as old and as consistent as the Church itself. What is new in our times is the "implosion" of the needs of the whole world into the Christian vocation of the individual.

The one dimension that is more pressing than any other in striving for the authenticity of a continuing Christian conversion in our times is the dimension of public responsibility, of responsibility to take a critical stance in relation to values and structures we take for granted, which make or mar the lives and happiness of great segments of the human population. Because this is so crucial within the Christian vocation in our times, so central to Christian conversion in our times, therefore it must become an acknowledged and privileged component in the sacrament of reconciliation, even in its individual form.

To recognize this in principle is much simpler than to implement it in practice. For both penitent and confessor there is a constant need to become aware, to "tune in" to the sufferings of the world, and to become informed and critical about the roles we as individuals, as interest groups, as political associations, as nations, play in those sufferings. This suggests a wider range of examination of conscience than most Catholics are accustomed to. It suggests something along the lines of the alternating gospel enquiries and social enquiries of the Jociste movement. The Christian responses are not blueprinted for us. Situations of suffering and deprivation always call for some kind of creative action, some kind of new solution, some experimental generosity, some humility and repentance in the face of the problem, some prayer acknowledging dependence and interdependence, some readiness for renunciations of privilege and power and wealth. Such situations of widespread and complex deprivation and oppression usually call for organized and communal action. But first there has to be the awakening of individual awareness, recognition, commitment.

The central question, therefore, is how this awareness and commitment can be aroused. There seem to be a number of starting ponts for any individual. One could, for instance, begin with one's own fears — fear perhaps of nuclear war breaking out, fear of burglaries or street violence, fear of losing one's job, fear of betrayal in certain relationships, and so forth. Each of these fears is realistically founded in social, political and economic conditions in the society. One might ask seriously where one stands in relation to these conditions, and would probably have to admit that violence is such a threat because we are among the privileged in a local or national or world population where many suffer acute want. One might pursue the matter and consider where one stands (or whether one has failed to take a stand) on the politics and economic choices that shape these conditions. And this in turn raises the question for all of us as to what we are willing to renounce in our standard of living, our status, power, privileges and freedoms, so that others may fully enjoy their share in God's creation and human history.

An alternate approach might be an examination of conscience from the local, national and international news in the daily newspaper. We might ask how Jesus would be likely to comment on those news items to a group of intimate disciples. We might agree at least momentarily to suspend the canons of customary worldly prudence and ask simply how these matters would be settled if God truly reigned in the world and if we all recognized one another as one family under God. We might play out the story of the Good Samaritan in our imaginations with Russian Communists playing the role of the Samaritan, or the story of the Pharisee and the Publican in the Temple with burglars and rapists and switchblade wielders playing the role of the Publican, or the drama of the Corinthian Eucharist in the presence of the starving peoples of Asia and Africa or the poor of Latin America.

But basic to all of this is one very simple and quite uncontroversial criterion of Christian conversion anywhere and at any time. This is the deepending and expansion of compassion, the increasing ability to say "we" in more intensive and more extensive ways, the growing willingness to share in the experience and struggle of the entire family of God. Authentic rootedness and gratitude should indeed overflow into the capacity for this, but at the same time to learn to be for others is to find oneself also coming to rest in a surer relationship with God. A genuine quest for God in silence and prayer is tested and testified not only in personal serenity but in the overflow of compassionate caring for others. But such compassionate caring expresses itself authentically in steps to become adequately informed and to be properly effective. The striving to be open to continuing conversion in the practice of individual confession can only be authentic if it maintains the tension of that compassion which is rooted in intimate converse with God and which expresses itself effectively in all the social, political and economic dimensions of human life.

The worldly, or social justice dimension of reconciliation is an inescapable element even in the reconciliation of individual penitents, but it receives its greater emphasis and scope in communal penance celebrations, whether with or without absolution. The communal celebrations offer the opportunity for this for two reasons. First of all they are in themselves community celebrations that lend themselves best to a more communitarian style of examination of conscience. This is the inspiration that has often been behind the groups practising *revision de vie.* When people come together solemnly to read scripture, meditate on it and try to put their own lives under its scrutiny it is to be expected that it is in the first place of their common life and common situations that they will be thinking.

Secondly, in a communal penance celebration it is necessary to select bible readings and prayers, responses and hymns for the congregational participation. And it is usual, and urged by the instructions, that there be a homily. In other words it is an opportunity to educate the conscience of the congregation. It is an opportunity to try to uncover some of those hidden dimensions of sin that can be so devastating in our lives precisely because we do not even recognize them as sin and therefore are not prompted to repent of them. Such are the distorted values, false priorities, unjust distributions of material resources and power and opportunity that riddle our life together in the world and in our immediate society. Such are racism, the arms race, the systematic crushing down of the poor and powerless, the national economy that ignores the destruction wreaked on others outside the country, and all the structures that we take for granted in the economy and the social and political sphere, which constitute in obvious or subtle ways the structures of sin.

This is in the tradition of the prophets of Israel.[4] It is in the tradition of the early church as we see it in the teachings of Jesus in the gospel of Luke and as we see it reflected in the stories and admonitions of the Acts of the Apostles and in the letters of the apostles, most notably in that of James.[5] It is in the tradition of the great Fathers of the Church, most spectacularly perhaps that of Ambrose of Milan.[6] It is in the tradition of the great movements of revival and renewal of fervor of every age in the Church.[7] But it has never been popular. Jesus, after all, suffered a political execution after an unfair trial as a political prisoner on the only accusation that could not easily be disproved, that he stirred up the people from Galilee even to Jerusalem. Early Christians were persecuted as a threat to the government and the good order of society. All Christian prophets have been accused

[4]*Cf.* John R. Donahue, S.J., "Biblical Perspectives in Justice"in John C. Haughey, S.J. ed. *The Faith That Does Justice* (Ramsey, N.J.: Paulist Press, 1977); and J.P.M. Walsh, S.J., "Lordship of Yahweh, Lordship of Jesus", in *Above Every Name*. And *cf.* Jose Miranda, *Marx and the Bible* (Maryknoll, N.Y.: Orbis Press, 1974).

[5]*Cf.* John C. Haughey, S.J., "Jesus as the Justice of God", and Donahue, *op. cit.*, in *The Faith That Does Justice.* See also John H. Yoder, *The Politics of Jesus* (Grand Rapids: Eerdman, 1972).

[6]*Cf.* William J. Walsh, S.J. and John P. Langan, S.J., "Patristic Social Consciousness — the Church of the Poor" in *The Faith That Does Justice.*

[7]*Cf.* Richard R. Roach, S.J., "Tridentine Justification and Justice" and David Hollenbach, S.J., "Modern Catholic Teachings Concerning Justice"in *The Faith That Does Justice.*

of not minding their own business, not staying within the boundaries of religion but meddling in affairs of state, matters of the economy and other "secular affairs". In the whole history of Christianity one can find few martyrs, even among all those whom the Church has canonized, of whom their persecutors and critics said that they were being put to death for religious reasons. On the contrary, it was always said that they constituted a threat to the good order of society, often that they were plotting against the state, were traitors to the national interest and so forth.

It is, then, not to be expected that sermons or penance celebrations on the themes of social justice, peace, and other questions of pervasive underlying assumptions and values running through the structures of our society, will be received in parishes without conflict or protest. Only specialized groups that have already become sensitized to the issues, perhaps by personal practical immersion in them, are likely to meditate on such matters together calmly and openly and in general agreement. On the one hand, this clearly can not be a reason for avoiding these themes, because the task of the Church is prophetic, and because reconciliation depends on conversion in societies as in individuals, a conversion likely to be costly for communities as for individuals. On the other hand, the task of the Church is reconciliation — a task of bringing its own members to peace with God, with one another, and with those about them in their immediate society and in the world at large. The peace that is sought is not the false peace of silencing the suffering of the powerless so that the surface of social life is unruffled. That is not peace or reconciliation, and clearly it has nothing of conversion about it. Yet what is sought *is* peace not hatred or bitterness or strife.

The practical challenge of prophetic witness within the churches for issues of social justice has never been an easy one. The goal is deep conversion of hearts expressing itself gently and spontaneously in a conversion of life and therefore of the structures of life in society. Such conversion of structures of life in society comes about not when some impose it on others but really only when the conversion is one of the community as such. Each can only contribute to this his or her own conversion expressed in gentler, more welcoming, less frightened and defensive, more generous, relations with others, especially with all who are needy no matter what the nature of their need.[8] The chief difficulty with this is, of course, that we are all so very much more needy than we are willing to admit, especially where the need is not in material things, and that we are all so very much more sinful and compromised in the false values of the world than prophets ought to be.

The challenge is to find a way of prophetic witness that is not compromised and invalidated from the outset by self-righteousness, judgemental attitudes, defensiveness against exposure of one's own weaknesses and sinfulness, blind spots of which one is not even aware while zealously preaching to others and exposing their false values. The problem in the celebration of community penance services is the powerful temptation to various interest groups in a parish to take over the planning of the readings and hymn and prayer texts with a view to converting others in the parish to their own way of thinking. This is frequently perceived as a strategy of psychological imperialism and countered in various ways, appropriate or inappropriate, which turn the parish (and perhaps the parish council) into warring factions. Different groups may, for instance, "seize power" in the planning of liturgies at various times and use these liturgies as a platform for their positions. This is hardly a constructive exercise in the conversion of the community.

This dilemma is not a hypothetical one. Many readers will respond to it with rueful memories, because the situation seems to be a very frequent occurrence in Catholic parishes today. It is one of those situations of which it might truthfully be said that with men it is indeed impossible but with God all things are possible, because it really does go to the heart of the human problem of sin and sinfulness. The heart

---

[8]On the intrinsic bond between the sacramental life of the Church and social justice, see David Hollenbach, S.J., "A Prophetic Church and the Catholic Sacramental Imagination" in *The Faith That Does Justice*; and John C. Haughey, S.J., "Eucharist at Corinth: You Are the Christ", in *Above Every Name*.

of the problem is self-centeredness so extensively inter-twined in human relationships, so firmly encrusted in the structures of society at all levels, so devastatingly pervasive but disguised in the churchly activities of Christians and subtly ensconced in the religious and spiritual identity of Christians, especially the most dedicated. It is so difficult to recognize the "enemy" within our own lives and attitudes and goals, that there is a permanent temptation to project the problem away from ourselves and locate it elsewhere.

But it is precisely for this reason that sacramental reconcil-iation in the Church can never be an individual affair only, but must be a community experience with personal, eccle-sial and wider social dimensions. The process of conversion has to move from inner conversion of hearts to exterior conversion of lives which involves relationships among peo-ple, and from person to person relationships within the Church communities to church structures, from local to larger, and from the transformation of Christian communi-ties and churches to a leavening influence in the society at large. One can not convert others in any literal sense, though one can antagonize them considerably and introduce a good deal of static onto the line of communication that is open between them and God. What one can do is to lay oneself open to being converted by the power of God's Word and Spirit in one's own life, in the hope that by changing one's own attitudes, behavior and relationships in the community one can minister to others by offering them a little more space and freedom for conversion of their attitudes, behav-ior and relationships. In this way one may indeed hope that such initiatives in the Kingdom of God among us will per-meate the world like leaven in the dough, so that the smoth-ering dead weight of sinfulness and surreptitious self-seeking might become a little lighter and airier and more workable.

What this seems to imply concerning communal penance celebrations, whether with or without absolution, with or without individual confessions, would seem to be closely analogous to what the tradition says about the role of the confessor in the celebration of reconciliation and conversion of an individual penitent. The first task is to pray with and for the others of the community. One prepares oneself for the meeting by becoming keenly aware of one's own personal sinfulness, and one begs God unceasingly for conversion for all of us, conversion from the evil we see, and from the evil so entrenched in us that we do not even begin to suspect it.

The second task is to listen with deep compassion. A good way to do this in a communal penance celebration, because sin is revealed in suffering, is by letting the suffering of others speak to us, by giving such suffering a voice in our assembly. This means in the first place always the suffering of Jesus which gathers into a startling presence at the center of human history, at the center of human experience, all the suffering and oppression that is hidden in the world, bringing it back into vivid remembrance as a parable of the human situation. But our liturgy and scriptures and tradition do not intend that the suffering of Jesus stand before us in meditation isolated and different from the people and world about us. It is intended precisely that we constantly bring the world and people and situations about us into juxtaposition with the suffering and self-gift of Jesus so that the parable may reshape our vision of reality, our imagining.[9]

To allow the suffering of others to speak in our assembly is a non-aggressive way of appealing for conversion of heart. Most of us have difficulty responding to a prophetic cry that attacks us directly with the message, "You are sinning; cease!" It is easier to listen to a cry that says, "I am in pain; help me", though the outcome of the message may be in practical terms exactly the same. Moreover, in the communal penance celebration it means that there is no need for some people in the parish to appear as the prophets accusing the others if all are listening to the cry of the suffering in the presence of Christ crucified. One can allow the suffering to utter their cry of pain in the midst of the assembly by stories

[9] *Cf.* Brian McDermott, S.J., "Power and Parable in Jesus' Ministry" in *Above Every Name.*

of particular individuals or groups, by descriptions, even by simple economic or political analyses. Very cautiously, with respect for the nature of God's speaking to consciences at the peak of inner freedom and not through emotional or other psychological manipulation—very cautiously one can allow those who are suffering to speak in a multimedia presentation. What is crucial is that it all has to be done by those who plan and prepare and organize in the spirit the tradition recommends, indeed requires, in the confessor —intense and humble awareness of one's own sinfulness including much yet hidden from oneself, prayer with and for the other, and deeply compassionate listening.

The third step or task in the communal penance celebration, as in the reconciliation of individual penitents, is the discernment of the spiritual situation — never "theirs" but "ours" — leading to prayer for God's forgiveness which is inseparable from the exigence of God's call to conversion. But this conversion can not happen all at once for a community, because conversion only happens within the freedom of human persons and at the peak of their freedom. Even taken individually, all of us have many areas of unfreedom and of struggling immature freedom. It is true that grace sets us free and is the freedom of our freedom, the unleashing or liberating of our own freedom. But it is also true that grace, precisely because it is the freedom of our freedom, does not overwhelm us but respects the spontaneity of our own responses. God always seems to be so much more willing to wait than we are, as the desert fathers knew when they rejected all that savored of the frantic or desperate. God always seems to be on desert time and never on city time.

But if this is so in individual conversion it is necessarily compounded in the conversion of communities. A community does not have a single conscience, a single freedom, a single memory or imagination, but many and varied and perhaps conflicting ones. Therefore a primary task of Church at all times and places and all levels of organization and grouping, from the simplest to the most complex, is to become in some measure of one mind and heart — to share imaginings, memories, feelings, longings and understandings. That means that the suffering which must be allowed to speak in any assembly must be also (and perhaps first of all) the suffering of those in the assembly speaking their hurt to one another in the context of prayer with and for one another which is a prayer for God's healing and forgiveness, the other side of the coin of repentance and conversion. This is indeed the proper sacrament of reconciliation of the community in its personal, ecclesial and wider social dimensions.

Recommended Reading

Thomas E. Clarke, S.J., ed. *Above Every Name: The Lordship of Christ and Social Systems* (Ramsey, N.J.: Paulist Press, 1980).

John C. Haughey, S.J., ed. *The Faith That Does Justice.* (Ramsey, N.J.: Paulist Press, 1977).

Daniel C. Durkin, O.S.B., ed. *Sin, Salvation and the Spirit* (Collegeville, Minn: Liturgical Press, 1979).

Joseph M. Champlin, *Preparing for the New Rite of Penance.* (Notre Dame, Ind.: Ave Maria Press, 1974).

CONCLUSION

RETROSPECT AND PROSPECT

Looking back over the history of the sacrament of penance one sees the Church responding to felt needs of changing times, sometimes almost imperceptibly and at other times with considerable questioning and conflict. One sees a polarity that is never resolved between the desire to implement the boundless compassion and welcome of God expressed in Jesus and the desire to maintain a community of the pure that is worthy of Jesus in its righteousness. The most that has been possible is to keep the two in tension. One also sees a polarity between the charisms of the living, growing, loving and sinning church community and the need for order and control through an institutional structure. This is never resolved either, but is kept in tension.

The rites that emerged from time to time reflect these tensions. At different times they were more public or more private, more severe or more lenient, more exceptional or more general. At times they stressed the juridical or the more personal, confession or satisfaction, what the penitent does or what the Church does, the holiness of the confessor or juridical designation. All that we can conclude is that there are many ways of celebrating a sacrament of reconciliation and that the Church, as the whole body of believers, has shaped them and can shape them to the needs of the members in changing times and places.

This brings to the fore again some persistent questions. How is the Church going to solve the challenge of growing numbers of Catholics who absent themselves from individual confession while it is still held to be mandatory in cases of serious sin and very strongly urged once a year in other cases? The institutional Church of the late patristic and early mediaeval times had to yield to the spontaneous movement of the people away from the discipline of canonical penance. In other words, is the Tridentine doctrine of the divine necessity of "integral confession", which was a mediaeval innovation, going to disappear again? If it disappears what basis is there for maintaining the necessity of priesthood for the ministry of sacramental reconciliation? Is the primary concern going to shift back to the holiness, experience, wisdom or skill of the minister rather than the power of orders and jurisdiction? Related to this is the question: is it becoming urgent for the well-being of the whole Church and the ongoing task of the redemption in the world, to acknowledge and appreciate the charism that many women have for this ministry of reconciliation? Likewise, is it perhaps more urgent for the well-being of the whole Church and the continuing work of redemption to try to draw the entire congregation of the faithful to periodic communal penance celebrations than to try to ensure that everyone confesses once a year?

Readers of this book may find themselves at this point with questions of their own about the future shape of reconciliation in the Church.